Overcoming Common Problems

OVERCOMING GUILT

Dr Windy Dryden

First published in Great Britain 1994
Sheldon Press, SPCK, Marylebone Road, London NW1 4DU

Second impression 1998

British Library Cataloguing-in-Publication Data
A catalogue record for this book is available from the British Library

ISBN 0–85969–686–3

Photoset by Deltatype Ltd, Ellesmere Port, Cheshire
Printed in Great Britain by Biddles Ltd, Guildford and King's Lynn

Contents

Preface

I frequently give lectures on mental health topics to the general public. The most challenging part of these lectures is the question and answer session that follows. The questions that people ask reveal the issues that are important to them and show their level of understanding on the topic being discussed.

Whenever I talk about guilt, the questions people raise indicate a lot of confusion about this troublesome emotion. Indeed, there is almost as much confusion in the professional literature on guilt! I decided to write this book to bring some order to this chaos. In particular, I wanted to make clear that we need to make a crucial distinction between guilt – which I regard as basically an unconstructive emotion – and its healthier counterpart, constructive remorse.

I also wanted to answer the many interesting questions I have been asked on guilt over the years by my audience and clients alike. This explains the question and answer format used throughout the book.

The illustrations are taken from my clients and included with their full permission. Any identifying material has been altered to protect confidentiality.

I wish to thank Caroline Dearden for her superb skills in helping to make this book intelligible, Joanna Moriarty for her editorial encouragement, and those clients and members of my lecture audience who have asked intelligent and challenging questions on the subject of this book – guilt.

Windy Dryden

1
What is Guilt?

In this opening chapter, I begin by defining guilt and showing how it applies to the seven deadly sins. I then go on to stress the central role that attitudes play in the guilt experience and examine the reasons behind guilt without any known cause. Finally, I argue that it is often not possible to avoid doing the wrong thing and look at ways of overcoming the feelings of guilt that arise from a preoccupation with past wrongdoings.

What is guilt?

In my opinion, guilt is a disturbed negative emotion that occurs under three major conditions.

First, you feel guilty when you interpret some action of yours as having broken a moral code or ethical principle, standard or value, and then bring a dogmatic attitude to your interpretation. As I will show throughout this book, the core of the guilt experience is that dogmatic attitude. Your interpretation that you have broken some code, for example, may involve you thinking that you have acted in an immoral or sinful way, experienced an immoral or sinful thought, felt an immoral or sinful impulse or had an immoral or sinful image.

You may also consider that you have failed to live up to some moral code or ethical principle, standard or value or that you have failed to discharge some important duty or responsibility. Again, in the guilt experience you bring a dogmatic attitude to this interpretation.

The second form of guilt occurs when you focus on the *consequences* of what you have done or what you have failed to do. In this type of guilt it is not your action, as such, that constitutes in your mind a violation of your moral code, but the

1

fact that in consequence of your action another person has been hurt in some way. In this form of guilt, the closer you are to the person whom you consider you have hurt (e.g. your parent, child or partner), the guiltier you feel. As in the first type of guilt, it is not just the interpretation that you have hurt somebody that causes your guilt: the central core of the guilt experience is again the dogmatic attitude that you bring to your interpretation that you have hurt another person.

The third type of guilt is different from the first two. In the first two types of guilt you either focus on something that you have done or not done or you focus on a negative consequence of your action (or failure to act). Both these types of guilt are rooted in particular episodes and that is why I refer to them as *episodic guilt*. In the third type of guilt, which I call *existential guilt*, you have a particular dogmatic attitude towards yourself which is focused on who you are in general, no matter what you have done or failed to do in life. This type of guilt is enduring and is not necessarily limited to particular episodes.

How does your analysis apply to the seven deadly sins?

Let's first consider what the seven deadly sins are. These sins are pride, avarice, lust, envy, gluttony, anger and sloth.

Let's take gluttony as an example. Here, you first make the interpretation that you have acted in a gluttonous manner, which in reality may or may not be true. When you are feeling guilty, however, you assume that it is true and then apply a dogmatic attitude to your interpretation. Again, it is not your gluttonous behaviour that leads directly to you feeling guilty but the attitude you have about your behaviour.

So, you stress the important role that our attitudes play in guilt. Why is this so important?

This is important because if you had a more flexible attitude about your unprincipled behaviour, you would experience what I call 'constructive remorse' rather than guilt.

Let me be very specific about the inflexible attitudes which are at the core of the guilt experience and compare these with the more flexible attitudes that are at the core of constructive remorse. Let's suppose that you have violated one of your ethical principles and have had lustful thoughts about your best friend's partner. According to my definition of guilt you bring the following dogmatic attitudes to your lustful thoughts. First, you believe that you absolutely must not have such thoughts. Second, you believe that it is terrible to have such thoughts. Third, you believe that you cannot stand having such thoughts. And finally, you believe that you are a bad person for having such thoughts. As I will show you later in this book, these dogmatic attitudes and the guilty feelings that stem from them make it very difficult for you to reflect in a sensible and objective manner about why you are having the thoughts in the first place. In other words, your feelings of guilt prevent you from understanding what these thoughts might mean about your relationship to your friend, his partner or your relationship with your own partner. You become so preoccupied with, for example, how bad you are that this stops you from learning more about yourself and the role that your lustful thoughts play in your life.

In contrast, when you experience constructive remorse about your lustful thoughts, you are holding the following flexible beliefs. First, you believe that while it may be preferable for you not to have these thoughts, there is no law of the universe which states that, as a human, you absolutely must not have them. Second, you believe that while it is bad and unfortunate that you have such lustful thoughts, it is not terrible or the end of the world. Third, you believe that while it is difficult to tolerate having such thoughts, they can be tolerated and there is no evidence that you cannot stand them. Finally, you have a more compassionate attitude towards yourself: you believe that you are a fallible human being rather than a bad person; you evaluate the thoughts, not yourself as a total human being.

These more flexible attitudes and the feelings of constructive remorse that stem from them do allow you to reflect on why you are having the lustful thoughts in the first place. Constructive remorse alerts you to the fact that there is something wrong in your life and allows you to think in a sensible and objective manner about what it is and what it might mean in the context of your life as a whole.

To summarize, guilt about violating or failing to live up to a moral code or ethical principle, or about hurting somebody close to you, is based on four dogmatic attitudes: demandingness, awfulizing, low frustration tolerance and self-blame. These attitudes are at the core of much emotional disturbance and, in the case of guilt, serve to prevent you from learning from your wrongdoings.

In contrast, when you feel constructively remorseful about violating or failing to live up to a moral code or ethical principle, or hurting somebody close to you, this feeling is based on a more healthy, flexible set of attitudes: a philosophy of desire, an anti-awfulizing attitude, a philosophy of high frustration tolerance, and a healthy philosophy of self-acceptance. These beliefs are healthy because they are logical, they are more consistent with reality and they help us to learn from our wrongdoings.

Some people say that they feel guilty for no good reason. Others say they feel guilty all the time. How do you explain this?

Let me first make the assumption that it is in fact guilt that these people are experiencing. I mention this because some people say that they feel guilty, where on further examination it turns out that they feel ashamed or depressed. Assuming that they are experiencing guilt, let me first take the case of those who say that they feel guilty for no good reason. Such people are not aware of committing any wrongdoing, but they have an enduring awareness of not acting morally or ethically. I demonstrate this point in my lectures on guilt. I ask members of the audience if they know of anyone who is sick or lonely. More than half the audience put their hands up. I then ask why they are listening to a lecture on guilt rather than looking after or comforting the sick or lonely person.

At any point in time you could be doing something more consistent with your moral or ethical values, but you have other interests: you wish to have a good time, pursue an important work project, or recover from the rigours of the day. Most people recognize that there is a time to act in a way that is obviously moral or ethical and there are also times when we need to pay attention to our other interests in life. (I do not wish to argue, however, that these interests completely lack moral or ethical content, only that they are less obviously moral or ethical.) However, if you feel guilty for no good reason, frequently you believe that you always have to act morally or ethically and if you do not, then you are a bad person. Such an attitude is frequently subconscious, which is to say that when you experience guilt, you are not aware that you are not living up to your ethical or moral standards. Thus, you may well be right when you say that you feel guilty for no good reason because you are not aware of why you are feeling guilty. However, if you ask yourself if there is anything you believe you should be doing at the time you feel guilty, then you can often become aware that you are in fact failing to live up to your moral code or ethical standards at that point in time.

Another reason why you may feel guilty for no good reason is that while you can see *objectively* that you have not done anything wrong, *subjectively* you hold yourself responsible for whatever has gone wrong. In this case you believe that if you have an involvement in some interaction which has gone wrong, for example, then you are totally to blame for it. However, if anyone were to ask you what you are guilty about, you may well not be able to point to anything that you have done (or not done) which transgresses your moral values.

Isobel is a young woman who has grown up with the belief that if anything goes wrong within a setting in which she has some involvement, however slight, then she is totally to blame for

5

this incident. Thus, Isobel believes that if she hires a video that the family does not like, then she is totally to blame for this situation because her family's negative feelings are *only* brought about by her wrongdoing for which she blames herself. In reality, however, such situations are never so simple. Thus, on further examination it transpires that she hired a videotape which she thought her family would like, but because there was some family crisis occurring at the time, nobody could fully concentrate on the video. When the family members said they weren't enjoying it, Isobel focused only on her own involvement in the situation and edited out completely the other factors that were impinging on the family members' lack of enjoyment of the film. Objectively, Isobel could see that she had not done anything wrong. Subjectively, she felt guilty because she believed that if she is involved in a situation, she is completely to blame for it. As this belief was outside Isobel's awareness, it seemed to her that she felt guilty for no 'good' reason.

It is always possible to focus on something that is going wrong in your environment with which you have some involvement and therefore, if you believe, like Isobel, that you are to blame for anything that goes wrong in which you have even the slightest involvement, then it is quite easy to see how you will feel guilty much, if not all, of the time.

Isobel, then, has what is called a sense of excessive responsibility. She dramatically overestimates her own responsibility in situations and dramatically underestimates the responsibility of others and the influence the environment has on life events. Thus, when she hired the videotape, she completely disregarded the impact of the crisis on the mood of the family members. She also disregarded the degree of responsibility that the other family members had concerning the choice of the videotape.

If you have a sense of excessive responsibility, you believe that you absolutely should be able to control events with which you are involved. Believing that you absolutely should be able to control events, when such events occur that are objectively beyond your control, you then blame yourself for not having the degree of control that you believe you absolutely must have. As I shall discuss later, this unrealistic demand for control over events is a feature of guilt experienced by those suffering from post-traumatic stress disorder when survivors believe that there was something they could have done to prevent the tragedy. However, in reality, human beings have limited control over their environment since their environment is populated with other people whom they cannot control and with impersonal objects which again they frequently cannot control.

Other people who say they feel guilty all the time are those who believe they have committed a 'terrible' sin, something for which they believe they cannot forgive themselves. Not only are they aware of this terrible sin, but they are also constantly aware of their own wickedness for committing the sin. These are people who say that their guilt is always with them. They may, for example, have cheated their employer out of a large sum of money, had an abortion, sexually abused a young child – in fact, anything which is a gross violation of their ethical and moral code. It is only when such people come to terms with themselves for committing their sin and begin to understand it, and to look at the mitigating factors involved, that they will feel constructively remorseful about what they have done, a feeling which will help them to integrate the experience into their lives and thus to move on without an accompanying sense of guilt. Otherwise, they will always be conscious, at some level, not only of what they have done, but also of how bad they are.

Other people who claim to feel guilty much or all of the time are those who have what I have called existential guilt. If you recall, these are people who grow up with the sense that they are bad through and through. No matter what they do in life, they cannot escape from the sense that they are by nature bad. Such people frequently, although not always, grow up in a family setting in which they have been regarded and treated as the 'black sheep' of the family. Family therapists have observed for many years that families may tend to scapegoat one individual so that the other family members, by focusing on the badness of that

7

individual, can be relieved of their own moral code violations or psychological problems. If you have grown up in a family in which you have been scapegoated, you will have a sense that the core of your being is bad. Indeed, this idea that you are bad has probably been reinforced day after day by the actions of other family members and by the way they interact with you. If you were to be asked what you feel guilty about, you would literally say, 'I don't know', and this will be true because your guilt is not related to any violation of your moral code. In your mind, you are just a bad person and that is that. Since you carry this identity around with you, you will therefore feel guilty much or all of the time.

Sometimes a feeling of enduring guilt is a sign of severe psychological disturbance such as severe depression. If you think this is the case, please do consult your GP who will be able to refer you for specialist help. I also advise those who have what I called existential guilt to seek psychotherapeutic help. There is no shame in doing so and a skilled therapist can, over time, help you to understand how you acquired this identity, how you maintain it and what you can do gradually to change it.

Is it possible to avoid doing the wrong thing?

The answer to this question is, it depends on the complexity of the situation that you find yourself in. Let's take a fairly simple example. You have, for a long time, admired a work colleague's fountain pen and wished you could afford to purchase a similar one for yourself. Your colleague leaves work one day leaving her pen in a place where many people will pass it. It would be so easy for you to take it and who would know? In this situation it is clear that if you steal the pen you are doing the wrong thing and that this can be avoided. If you are tempted to steal it, you need to ask yourself what you are telling yourself in being so tempted. The answer will probably be 'Because I really want the pen, I absolutely must have it'. If you realize that this demanding philosophy is present in your thinking then you can challenge it by asking yourself a number of questions.

- Why must I have what I want? [Answer: You don't have to have what you want.]

- Can I stand being deprived of something that I really want? [Answer: Yes, of course you can, although it is uncomfortable.]

- Do I really want to act in a way which contradicts my moral standards? [If you think hard about it, the answer to this question will probably be no.]

If you can appreciate that you hold an irrational belief which is strongly encouraging you to do the wrong thing, then you can challenge this belief and live with your deprivation, but be pleased that you have not transgressed your moral values.

However, there are many situations in life when such clear-cut situations do not exist. You are frequently faced with carrying out different duties which conflict with one another. For example, if you tend to your spouse, you may be neglecting your parents; if you look after your children, you may be neglecting your spouse. So it is important to accept the grim reality that by doing one good thing, you may, at the same time, be doing something which, from your ethical standpoint, is wrong. Therefore, it is important to accept the fact that frequently you will do something wrong while acting in the service of your other ethical values.

In a recent newspaper article, a woman who works for a large company related how she simultaneously tried to work and look after her husband who suffered from multiple sclerosis. On reading the article, it is clear that this woman is doing a sterling job on all fronts under very difficult circumstances. Yet she admits to feeling guilty when she is at work because she is not caring for her husband, and she feels guilty when she's caring for her husband because she is not at work. She is in a constant state of guilt and anxiety, feelings which may lead her to experience 'carer burnout', a state of depletion and emotional exhaustion when a carer tries to care simultaneously for a sick relative and carry out other significant duties.

If this woman acknowledges that she cannot avoid doing the wrong thing – in the sense that she cannot simultaneously satisfy two different ethical values – and gives up her demand that she must not do the wrong thing, she will be able to organize her life without guilt. This would involve her looking at the different pressures in her life, prioritizing them and drawing healthy boundaries around these different activities. Thus, when she is at work, she could remind herself that she is living up to one of her ethical principles rather than focusing on the other ethical principle which she is violating, that is, failing to care for her husband.

To put it another way, when this woman is at work she could remind herself that she *should* be at work and that she shouldn't be caring for her husband, because that is the decision she has made in an overall appraisal of her life situation. Similarly, when she is looking after her husband she could remind herself that she should be looking after her husband and she shouldn't be at work because again she has chosen at that time to care for her husband. If she doesn't surrender her guilt-creating philosophy, her only other possible solution is to clone herself! Thus, when one of her cloned selves is looking after her husband, the other of her cloned selves is simultaneously at work. This is what I call the 'futile doppleganger' solution. I hope you can see that this is obviously a ridiculous attempt to solve what is quite clearly a difficult situation.

A final word on the question of whether you can avoid doing the wrong thing. It is important to recognize that your values change over time. Thus, you may do what you consider to be the right thing at one point in time, but several years later when you look back from a different value perspective, you may conclude that you have done the wrong thing. If you make yourself feel guilty about this past 'wrongdoing', what you are really demanding is that you should not have acted in the way you did *then* because you *now* consider it to be wrong. In trying to overcome feelings of guilt, it is important to be clear and honest with yourself about what your values were and how you were thinking at the time you chose to do something. Don't make the mistake of judging past actions by your present standards and attitudes.

In summary, when you are faced with fairly simple situations where one course of action is clearly wrong, you can avoid doing the wrong thing if you look carefully at the irrational beliefs that are leading you to consider committing some wrong. Here it is important to identify, challenge and change these irrational beliefs if you are to avoid doing wrong. However, frequently you are faced with quite complex situations which seem to divide your loyalties. In trying to act in a way that is consistent with one set of values, you may be doing something which violates a different set of values. In such situations, you cannot avoid doing the wrong thing. Finally, it is important to appreciate that your values change over time, and that an action which you considered to be right at one point in time, you may now judge to be wrong. In such situations it is important for you to appreciate the frame of mind that you were in then and the set of values that you held then. Do not judge your past actions by your current values and frame of mind.

I am preoccupied with something I have done in the past and still feel guilty about, and I constantly go over this act in my mind. Can you help me stop this preoccupation?

When you focus on past behaviour which you consider was a violation of your moral code or an instance where you harmed somebody, your basic belief is probably 'I absolutely should not have done what I did'. It may well be that your constant preoccupation is of the kind where you constantly review the episode in your mind in search of how you could have stopped yourself acting in the way that you did. If this is the case, your thinking is likely to be peppered with statements such as 'if only I'd have known then what I know now, I wouldn't have acted in the way that I did', or, 'surely there could have been some way I could have stopped myself from doing what I did at the time'.

The idea that you absolutely shouldn't have done what you did is, when you think about it, a preposterous one. Your action, at the time you carried it out, was based on the way you saw and thought about the situation at that time. We could say that all the conditions were in place for you to act in the way that you did. You were in a particular situation, you viewed that situation in a certain way, and the way you thought about the situation led you to act in the way you did. Thus to argue, as I think you are doing, that you absolutely shouldn't have acted the way that you did, is tantamount to making a demand that reality at that time should not have existed. What we do know about reality is that it does exist and that since all the conditions are in place for it to exist, we could even say that it should exist. Certainly, you could have acted differently if you had the knowledge then that you presumably have now, and indeed wouldn't it be a glorious world if we could travel in a time machine back into the past and undo our actions, based on our subsequent understanding and knowledge of why we acted in the way we did. However, this is impossible and you are demanding the impossible. You are demanding that you should have acted then in the way that you would want to act now. This cannot be achieved, so rather than berating yourself in the way that you seem to be doing, you need to do the following:

- acknowledge that you acted in a way that you consider to be morally wrong;
- identify, challenge and change your guilt-creating demands, namely, that you absolutely shouldn't have acted in the way that you did and that you are a bad person for so doing;
- realize that you should have done what you did, since your action was based on the situation you were in and the beliefs that you had about that situation.

I repeat – you should have acted in exactly the way that you did, given what was in your mind at that time. Realize, therefore, that when you are preoccupied about a past event, you are demanding that you should have known then what you know now. That would be nice but that is humanly impossible.

A similar belief, and one that is held by someone who witnessed a situation where he chose not to get involved or by someone who did involve herself in some kind of rescue but was able to help only certain people and not others, is expressed as: 'I absolutely should have done what I did not do.' Again, this is humanly impossible.

For example, if you witness a robbery and choose not to intervene to stop it, your inaction can be explained by the thoughts and feelings you had at the time. Let's suppose that you were afraid because you believed that if you had intervened, you would have been hurt and that was something that you did not want to experience. That way of looking at the situation and your associated fear, explains why you did not intervene. It is useless to go back and say that you should have done something which you could not have done, given the way you were thinking and feeling at the time.

Similarly, if you successfully rescued someone from a disaster and failed to rescue somebody else, your actions at the time can again be explained by the thoughts you had at that time which influenced your decision to act in a certain way rather than in another way. Thus, if you find yourself saying 'If only I had taken time to think, I would have realized that there was a way I could have saved both people', this way of thinking is a variation on the theme 'I absolutely should have done what I didn't do'. Let me again reiterate that, given the conditions that existed at the time, there is no way you could have acted any differently from the way you did. Maybe, faced with the same situation now, based on your knowledge of what happened in the past, you would choose to act differently. But there is certainly no reason why you absolutely should have acted differently then. Again, if you believe that you absolutely should have known what you didn't know at the time, this again is demanding the impossible. What you knew at the time was based upon what you chose to pay attention to at the time and this cannot be undone.

In both these situations, as you challenge your beliefs, 'I absolutely shouldn't have done what I did' and 'I absolutely should have done what I did not do', please recognize that you are demanding that reality should not have been reality. If we know anything about past reality, it is that it should have existed because all the conditions were in place for it to have existed. Realize that you can learn from your experiences and choose to act differently in the future. But you cannot go back to the past and put right what you failed to do then. In short, you cannot rewrite history!

There is a final situation that I wish to discuss which is relevant to this theme of being preoccupied with your past wrongdoings. Sometimes you may bring a present moral code to bear on a past action performed at a time when you did not believe in the same code. Thus, even though you did not consider yourself to be guilty of a wrongdoing in the past, now, looking back, you consider that you acted wrongly and believe that you absolutely shouldn't have done that. Once again, it is important to realize that your behaviour *then* was determined by the way you viewed the situation *then*, which included the moral code that you held *then*. To feel guilty about that action now, is to believe that you should have had the moral code *then* that you have *now*. This is another example of your attempt to rewrite history by projecting your current values onto your past behaviour. Rather than try to do the impossible, why not accept the fact that you acted in the way that you believed was right then, even though you now consider it to be wrong.

In short, whenever you are preoccupied with some wrong-doing in the past, realize that what you are trying to do is to undo what cannot be undone. Accept this grim reality, give up your demands about it, and learn from the experience so that you can concentrate on modifying what you can change, namely your future behaviour, and give up trying to change what you cannot change, namely your past behaviour.

2
What are the Effects?

In chapter 2, I discuss some of the major emotional effects of guilt, such as fear, depression and loneliness. I explore the ways in which people who feel guilty tend to act, including those who develop obsessive-compulsive problems to avoid guilt.

I understand more clearly from what you say that guilt has negative effects, but I still think that experiencing guilt helps to draw our attention to the fact that something is wrong in our lives. After all, if you do not feel guilty you don't know that there is anything wrong. Surely guilt can be helpful in this respect?

Certainly some authorities think so. For example, Tony Gough, in his otherwise excellent book *Don't Blame Me* (Sheldon Press, 1990), says that guilt is a friendly warning that something is wrong and needs attention (p. 33). Lindsay-Hartz who has done a lot of research into guilt says that guilt is helpful since it (a) highlights our moral standards, (b) shows that we have control by reminding us that we could have done something differently, and (c) supports the value of reconciling ourselves with others and being forgiven. I would have no argument with these authorities if they were to substitute the words 'constructive remorse' for the word 'guilt'. The difficulty with much of the psychological research and writing on guilt is that it does not discriminate between what I call unhealthy guilt (that which stems from rigid philosophies towards ourselves and our behaviour) and constructive remorse (which stems from a more flexible compassionate attitude towards ourselves and our behaviour). This means that you can never be clear whether an authority on guilt is referring to unhealthy guilt or constructive remorse. This confusion is one of the major reasons why I decided to write a book on guilt.

To make my own position clear: my view is that guilt (that unhealthy emotion stemming from rigid philosophies towards ourselves and our behaviour) does have the capacity to be helpful in drawing our attention to the fact that something is wrong. However, the negative effects tend to overwhelm any potentially positive effects that guilt may have as an early-warning system. In this sense, guilt is equivalent to having your smoke alarm going off in your house while at the same time your kitchen blows up. The fact that your kitchen has blown up will of course distract you from the smoke alarm.

By contrast, constructive remorse serves as a smoke alarm without the explosion in your kitchen. Since remorse stems from a flexible, non-demanding, non-blaming philosophy, it alerts you to the fact that there is something wrong and needs attention; it alerts you to the fact that you may have transgressed your moral standard; it shows you that you have more control than you think you have in the situation because you can learn from your past mistakes; and it supports the value of being reconciled with others and asking for forgiveness if in fact you have 'sinned' against them. So, constructive remorse does all that Tony Gough and Lindsay-Hartz claim as healthy in guilt, but it does this without the overwhelmingly negative effects of guilt which only serve to distract you from the healthy warning signs that something is wrong and needs your attention.

A final consideration here is that guilt interferes with your taking an objective view of the situation in all its complexity, whereas remorse helps you to make an objective appraisal of the factors involved. When you are feeling guilty, you tend to overestimate your degree of responsibility for a situation and minimize the impact of other factors that do not involve you. To use a slightly different analogy, guilt is like a fire alarm which, when it goes off, indicates that there is a fire throughout the entire building; remorse on the other hand, is like a fire alarm which, when it goes off, pinpoints exactly the source of the fire.

16

Sandra had promised her friend that she would take the friend's dress to the dry cleaners ready for the friend to wear that weekend at an office party. Unfortunately, Sandra forgot all about the dress and when she discovered that she had broken her promise she became very guilty. She blamed herself because she believed that under all circumstances she must always keep her promise. If Sandra had experienced constructive remorse about her broken promise and had accepted herself for being a fallible human being who had done the wrong thing, she would have been able to think more clearly about the situation and pinpoint the source of the problem; this would have helped her to make amends. She would have realized that her forgetfulness had led to some inconvenience for her friend and would have apologized to her and made various suggestions about how they could both rectify the situation in a joint problem-solving session. Such remorse would have enabled Sandra to be objective, to pinpoint the source of the problem and to take effective means to rectify it. However, Sandra was feeling guilty. Under the influence of guilt, she concluded that her friend would be furious with her and that the friend would go to the party and have a lousy time which would be all Sandra's fault. Because of her guilt and the kinds of negative interpretations she made, Sandra told her friend, in an attempt to absolve herself of all responsibility, that the bag she had put the dress in was stolen. However, this only compounded the problem because Sandra now felt guilty not only for breaking her promise but also for lying to her friend. So guilt, rather than alerting Sandra that there was something wrong, encouraged her to commit yet another wrongdoing. This second wrongdoing was committed by Sandra in a futile attempt to deal with her initial feelings of guilt about the broken promise.

As this example shows, constructive feelings of remorse help you to pinpoint more effectively what is wrong in a situation and encourage you to rectify the situation in an objective manner. However, guilt, while it may alert you to the fact that there is

17

something wrong, doesn't help you to pinpoint accurately the source of the problem. Furthermore, it leads you to make all kinds of negative inferences and interpretations about the situation for which you consider yourself totally responsible and to blame. Finally, guilt tends to lead you to commit further wrongdoings for which you then proceed to condemn yourself. In other words, guilt brings you a whole host of self-defeating distractions which are by and large absent when you are feeling remorseful.

What other emotions do people experience when they feel guilty?

Bruce Narramore, who has written extensively on the relation-ship between psychology and theology in guilt, has argued that people who feel guilty tend also to experience three other types of feelings. These feelings together comprise what he calls the 'punitive self'. First, when you experience guilt you also tend to be *afraid*. Since you consider yourself to be a bad person when you feel guilty, you may also tend to think that you deserve to be punished. Thus, you feel frightened that punishment may be meted out to you. You may consider that this punishment will come directly from God or that God may arrange for you to be punished by other people or by adverse life conditions. In addition, when you are feeling guilty and fear that you may be punished, you may be afraid that you may punish yourself in some way, for example by harming yourself physically.

Incidentally, people who fear punishment from God tend to practise a form of religion, or be brought up in a religious environment, in which the concept of God is of a deity who is strict, stern and vindictive.

The second major emotion that people who feel guilty often experience is *depression*. Self-blame, which is a common attitude in the guilt experience is also, as Paul Hauck has noted, a central attitude in depression. When you are feeling guilty your self-blame takes the form of statements that you are bad or wicked. You may also consider yourself to be worthless, an attitude that tends to lead you to feel depressed rather than guilty. People who experience existential guilt (those who believe their core identity is one of badness and wickedness independent of how they behave), also tend to feel depressed because they feel hopeless about the future. They literally believe there is no way that they can rescue themselves from their inherent badness.

The third major feeling that people who feel guilty experience is *loneliness*. When you consider yourself to be a bad person you also assume that other people will reject you because they will see how bad you are. Thus, you tend to stay away from people and isolate yourself from social activities. As a result you experience a sense of loneliness, a painful emotional state, but one which you prefer when you are feeling guilty to taking the risk of mixing with people and being rejected by them.

However, when you experience constructive remorse rather than guilt you are far less likely to experience fear, depression and loneliness. This is because you do not consider yourself to be a bad person for breaking your moral code; you accept yourself as a fallible human being rather than one who is damnable; and you do not believe that you will be punished for your so-called sins. Furthermore, when you accept yourself rather than blame yourself, you will feel sad about your moral code violation rather than depressed.

Finally, when you are feeling remorseful about your wrongdoing rather than guilty about it, you are far less likely to believe that other people will reject you. Since you do not consider yourself to be a bad person for your wrongdoing, you are less likely to think that other people will consider you to be a bad person. The threat of rejection in your mind is substantially lessened, and you are more likely to engage with others and less likely to isolate yourself from them. Finally, if guilt, fear, depression and loneliness constitute what Narramore calls 'the punitive self', constructive remorse, concern and sadness constitute what may be called the 'compassionate self'. Those who develop a compassionate attitude towards themselves for their wrongdoings are more likely to experience remorse when they break their moral code than guilt.

What action do people tend to take when they feel guilty?

In a book that I have written with my American colleague Joseph Yankura entitled *Counselling Individuals: A Rational-Emotive Handbook* (Whurr Publishers, 1993), we make the point that when you experience an emotion you also have a tendency to act in a certain way. This doesn't mean that you will in fact carry out the action, just that you have a tendency to do so. Thus, when you experience guilt, you may have a tendency to act in a number of different ways. First, if a component of your self-blame is that you think that you deserve to be punished for your wrongdoings, then you may have a tendency to harm yourself in some way. For example, you may wish to inflict pain on yourself by banging your head up against a wall, cutting yourself or stubbing cigarettes out on your skin. In fact, some people do this. If you are a person who inflicts physical pain on themselves when you are feeling guilty, it is important that you seek professional help since while you may not wish to inflict permanent or terminal harm on yourself, this may be the tragic consequence of your self-harming behaviour.

Second, when you believe that you have committed a wrong-doing which has led to other people being harmed or hurt, you may seek out the other person and beg them to forgive you. As I will presently show you, this is different from an adult–adult exchange in which you apologize to the other person for your wrongdoing and, from a position of self-acceptance, ask for forgiveness. Rather, since you consider yourself to be a bad person, you may literally go on your knees and plead with the other person to forgive you.

Third, when you feel guilty, you may believe that you are undeserving of pleasure. Consequently, you may seek to punish yourself by staying away from activities which are enjoyable for you until you have expiated your sin. If you are like some people, you may believe that even though you may have expiated your sin by going to confession or being forgiven by other people, you believe that you need to carry out a penance and may ban yourself from enjoyable activities for a period, undertake to fast in order to cleanse yourself from your sin or undertake some very unpleasant activity which may benefit somebody else. In this latter example, you do this, not necessarily because you wish to help those less fortunate than yourself but to suffer for your sins.

The fourth major way that you tend to act when you feel guilty is to engage in activities which help you to forget about your wrongdoing. Thus, you may deliberately throw yourself into work to forget, or you may drink yourself into oblivion. You may believe implicitly that the only way you can get over your guilt is to forget about what you have done. As you can appreciate, this works only in the short term and may lead you to become addicted to your work or to become an alcoholic. If you believe that you have a serious drinking problem which is motivated by your wish to forget some wrongdoing, consult your doctor and ask for a referral to a specialist alcohol counselling service.

When you experience constructive remorse rather than guilt you may have a different set of action tendencies and you will probably act in a more constructive manner. There is also far less chance of your wishing to harm yourself since you do not consider yourself to be a bad person who deserves, in this case, self-punishment. You are also far less likely to deprive yourself of pleasure because you do not consider yourself to be undeserving of such pleasure. When you experience remorse, you recognize that you have done something wrong, you seek to put it right if you can, and since you accept yourself as a fallible human being, you are able to go about your life in a normal way, having learnt from the experience and resolved to minimize the chance of acting in a similar way in the future.

Finally, when you experience remorse rather than guilt, you take responsibility for your actions and, since you accept yourself for your wrongdoing, you are more likely to think about what you

21

did and learn from it, rather than engage in distracting activities designed to help you forget about what you've done.

I know guilt doesn't help me and that is why I kick myself whenever I feel guilty. It is as if I give myself two problems for the price of one. What can I do?

Actually, when you kick yourself for feeling guilty you not only give yourself two problems for the price of one, you frequently give yourself three problems for the price of one. Let me give you an example.

Stuart came to me for counselling to help him overcome his problems of anger, in that he would frequently have a temper tantrum when his partner deprived him of what he saw as his rights. Thus his first emotional problem was anger. However, Stuart also made himself guilty about his anger because he believed (a) that anger was a bad, unconstructive emotion, and (b) that he absolutely should not be angry and that he was a bad person for so doing. So his second emotional problem was guilt. I helped him to see that his feelings of guilt significantly interfered with his understanding the sources of his anger. I suggested that he first worked towards becoming constructively remorseful about his anger, since this would more likely help him to understand and deal with the underlying determinants of his anger.

Stuart was a bright and able man who quickly understood the point that I made to him about the self-defeating aspects of his guilt. However, inadvertently, realizing that his guilt was self-defeating led Stuart to give himself a third emotional problem. How did he do this? When Stuart thought back over his past episodes of anger he immediately made himself guilty. Realizing what I had said about the self-defeating nature of guilt, Stuart made himself angry about his guilt in the following way: 'I now realize that guilt is interfering with my attempts to overcome my anger problem and as such it is self-defeating and a block to my progress. Therefore, I absolutely should not make myself guilty. I am still doing so and therefore I am a stupid, incompetent person for continuing to make myself feel guilty.' Like the questioner, Stuart realized that guilt didn't help him and he metaphorically kicked himself whenever he felt guilty. Thus his third problem was anger at himself.

Since Stuart had now three problems rather than the one he sought help for, my counselling task was initially made more difficult. However, I helped Stuart first by encouraging him to accept himself for making himself feel guilty. I showed Stuart that even though his guilt was self-defeating, he was a fallible human being who occasionally would act in a self-defeating way. Then I helped him overcome his guilt by encouraging him to realize that while his expressions of anger were defeating both to himself and to his relationship, and were in that sense 'wrong', there was no reason why, as a fallible human being, he absolutely shouldn't do such wrong things; once again he could accept himself as a fallible human being who was doing the wrong thing, rather than condemn himself as a bad person. Only then could I help him to overcome his original presenting problem, namely anger.

If you have followed me so far in this book and agree that guilt is an unhealthy negative emotion, please also recognize that you may, like Stuart, become angry with yourself whenever you do 'the wrong thing' and feel guilty. The only way to overcome this problem is to work on fully accepting yourself as a fallible human being who may occasionally do the wrong thing and so make yourself feel guilty. This more self-accepting and compassionate attitude towards yourself for experiencing guilt will then help you to understand the sources of guilt and help you to overcome these and work towards feeling more constructively remorseful.

I've been told that guilt plays a role in obsessive-compulsive problems. Can you explain this?

Guilt plays a central role in one particular form of obsessive-compulsive behaviour, namely checking. Here you compulsively check that electrical appliances are unplugged, that gas cookers are turned off and that doors are locked. You engage in these behaviours compulsively, before you are prepared to leave your house. You engage in these activities repetitively and, in severe cases, you may do so for several hours. In order to understand the role that guilt plays in obsessive-compulsive checking, it is important for you to realize that you are taking excessive responsibility for events within your personal domain or psychological territory. Interestingly, if you engage in obsessive-compulsive checking, you are able to reduce your checking behaviour if someone you trust is prepared to take responsibility for ensuring that things have been checked. In addition, when you move into a new environment, which you have not yet defined as your psychological territory, for instance, if you are admitted to hospital, then you are able greatly to reduce your obsessive-compulsive checking until you begin to define your new environment as part of your personal domain over which you have personal responsibility.

This phenomenon of excessive responsibility for events occurring in environments which you define as your personal domain, explains why you may only be able to go on holiday for a brief period. For if you stay in that new environment for long enough, you begin to feel comfortable in that environment, regard it as part of your psychological territory and your obsessive-compulsive checking returns.

If you check in an obsessive-compulsive way, you are likely to hold the following beliefs:

- I am totally responsible for what goes on in my environment;
- if any harm or damage occurs in that environment that I could have theoretically prevented by my checking behaviour,

I am a bad person for not doing what I absolutely should have done, namely check.

Guilt also plays an important role in obsessive thinking. For example, over the years I have counselled several upstanding Christian women who will not go to church because they have experienced a forbidden thought or desire whilst in church. Thus, they may think of having sex with Jesus Christ, become horrified at their thoughts, believe that they absolutely must not think such thoughts and that they are wicked individuals for so doing. The belief that they absolutely must not think such forbidden thoughts or have such forbidden desires tends to increase these thoughts and desires. From their perspective, therefore, the only way that they can rid themselves of their thoughts is to stop attending church. However, they also feel guilty about this because they believe that it is wrong not to attend church and that they absolutely must not do the wrong thing and that they are wicked individuals for their wrongdoing.

It is a well-known psychological fact that if you try to control your thoughts and try to prevent yourself from thinking in a certain way, these attempts increase such thoughts. Let me underscore this point by inviting you to engage in a brief experiment. Close your eyes and think of a pink elephant. Now tell yourself that you absolutely must not think of a pink elephant. I think you will see that if you believe that you absolutely must not think of a pink elephant, the one thing that you are thinking of is – a pink elephant!

If you are to be helped to overcome your obsessive thinking, you need to realize that you do not have perfect control over your thoughts and quite frequently you will think incongruous thoughts, particularly in environments where you wouldn't expect to have such thoughts. Thus, you may have aggressive and sexual impulses and related thoughts in church, primarily because church is a holy place where you wouldn't expect such thoughts to occur.

Thoughts are different from impulses, which in turn are different from acts, which themselves are not equivalent to your total self. Thus, if you believe that you are a wicked person for having a wicked thought you think that the very presence of the thought makes you a wicked person. Whereas in reality, a so-called wicked thought is something that you may not have control over, particularly in environments where you may not expect them. Furthermore, having such thoughts does not mean that you will have the impulse to act on them. Even if you do have the impulse to act on them, it doesn't mean that you will act on them. And if you do, in fact, act on your impulses, that is an indication that you have a psychological problem rather than proof that you are a damnable, wicked individual.

Guilt also plays a role if you are obsessive-compulsive and do not fulfil your potential at work. If this is the case, you'll probably avoid taking on extra responsibility even though you are quite capable of doing so. You avoid this because you believe that if you have added responsibility, you absolutely must discharge it properly and that you are a bad person if you fail to do what you absolutely have to do. Believing that you absolutely have to do the right thing can also explain why you may often fail to complete tasks. If this is your problem you probably find yourself moving from task to task leaving each one uncompleted. Here you believe that if you do complete the task then you are responsible for it and, since you have to do it perfectly well, you are a bad person if you fail properly to discharge your responsibility. However, failing to complete tasks does not mean that you do not experience guilt, for you may also believe that failing to finish a task is evidence of irresponsible behaviour, and you absolutely must not act irresponsibly and are a bad person for so doing.

Finally, if you tend to be obsessive-compulsive, guilt might explain why you find it difficult to show your anger. For you believe that if you show your anger towards another person, you may cause that other person harm, something which you believe you absolutely must not do and that you are a bad person for so doing.

If obsessive-compulsive problems significantly interfere with your life, it is important to recognize that you need professional help. Obsessive-compulsive problems are not a sign of mental illness, other than in extreme circumstances, and can be helped through appropriate treatment. Ask your doctor for a referral to a psychiatrist or clinical psychologist if your obsessive-compulsive problems significantly interfere with you living a happy life.

Does excessive responsibility play a role in guilt other than in obsessive-compulsive disorders?

If you routinely feel guilty, you tend to attribute more responsibility to yourself for your moral code violations and their consequences and for harming other people than is warranted. The origins of this excessive responsibility lie in a childhood tendency for you to see yourself as the centre of the universe so that whatever happens in your environment can be attributed to you. Such excessive responsibility is, in other words, a natural stage of human development. While most people develop a more healthy and realistic perspective on personal responsibility which takes into account all the other factors which may influence the events with which they are involved, it may well be that, if you still as an adult feel excessive responsibility, you have failed to develop beyond this egocentric position. In addition, if you take excessive responsibility, you may well have grown up in a family in which you learned that whatever went wrong in the family was your fault.

While some people have an enduring style of assuming an excessive amount of responsibility for negative events in which they are involved, there are some dramatic occurrences which influence most of us so that we take far more responsibility about an outcome than is warranted. Barbara Fowles, in discussing her experiences of working with parents and families of children with illnesses and handicaps, notes that these people would almost invariably say at some point about the child and her disability: 'You see, I feel it is my fault; as if I had caused it by my own badness', and they sometimes add, 'It isn't fair that she should suffer for my wrong.'

In such stark circumstances those who take excessive responsibility also assume that if only they had acted in a certain way then they could have prevented the bad situation from happening. Thus in Fowles' example, the parents of children with the illness or handicap assume that they could have done something to prevent this from happening. While such people say, when questioned, something like 'I know this is irrational, but I think it anyway', they really believe implicitly that they *should* have far greater control over their environment than is, in fact, possible. It is extremely unlikely that a child's handicap is caused by some moral sin that the parents may have committed and indeed it is unlikely that they could have done anything to prevent the handicap, given the strong genetic basis of many such handicaps. In all probability, the tendency to take excessive responsibility for the negative events with which you are involved is closely linked to the idea that you absolutely should have much greater control over your life than in fact you do have.

In order, then, to give up a style of thinking which involves you taking an excessive amount of responsibility, you need first to give up the idea that you have a very large degree of control over your environment. By saying this, I do not mean to imply that you have very little control over your environment, rather that your degree of influence over events in your life is only a part of the large and complex number of factors that need to be taken into account when determining how much personal responsibility to take for a negative situation occurring.

In *Don't Blame Me* Tony Gough argues that it is sensible to think of responsibility along a continuum. He devised a continuum of responsibility which has five main points, ranging from a situation where you have 0% responsibility for an event, 25% responsibility for an event, 50% responsibility for an event, 75% responsibility for an event, to a situation where you have 100% or total responsibility for an event. If you have an excessive sense of responsibility you will frequently take 75% or, more usually, 100% responsibility for a negative event. Interestingly, if this is true of you, you will rarely take 100% responsibility for a positive outcome!

My own approach to helping people divide up responsibility fairly amongst the large number of factors that are potentially responsible for an event involves dividing up a pie. Let me give you an example of the way I typically use this with my clients.

Maureen was given a set of keys to look after by a workmate. She mislaid these keys and feared that somebody at her workplace would find them and use them to open a locker to steal some important equipment. I asked her to imagine that the valuable equipment had been stolen and asked her who was responsible for this. She answered 'Of course, I am'. I replied, 'So you were the one who took the keys, opened the locker and stole the equipment, were you?' This took Maureen aback, because she hadn't even considered that another person could have been responsible for the potential theft.

What is Maureen responsible for here? I believe that Maureen is responsible for mislaying the keys. If somebody at work took the keys and opened the locker and stole the equipment, that person is responsible for the theft; Maureen is not. In discussing this with Maureen, and using my 'dividing the pie' approach, I helped her shift from the position where she took 100% responsibility for the theft (or all of the pie) to a situation where she took 30% responsibility for the theft (or less than a third of the pie), leaving the thief to take 70% responsibility for it. Although I considered that 30% responsibility for the theft was still rather high, it was far less than the total responsibility that Maureen had taken before our conversation. As it happened, when she went to work the next day, one of her colleagues had in fact found the keys and handed them in to security. With a wry smile on my face I said, 'Oh, I suppose you are totally responsible for the recovery of the keys too, Maureen.' We both laughed heartily at the irony of this remark!

In closing, I wish to discuss a rare and sad condition to demonstrate the lengths taken by some people who tend to take excessive responsibility for the negative events in their environment. When these people hear that a crime has been committed in their neighbourhood, they believe that they have committed it. Their philosophy is: if a bad event happens within my neighbourhood, it is totally my fault. This belief leads them to confess compulsively to crimes that they have not in fact committed.

The Chief Rabbi, Jonathan Sacks, on a recent radio programme, sensibly said that 'we are responsible within our sphere of influence'. While the vast majority of people would see quite clearly that those who compulsively confess to crimes that are committed within their neighbourhood are taking responsibility far beyond their sphere of influence, it is important to recognize that these people truly believe that these crimes are within their personal domain and that therefore they are responsible for them. I need to stress that this compulsive tendency to confess to crimes is a sign of a serious psychological condition and one that requires psychiatric treatment. Please see your doctor if you believe that this applies to you.

While I have shown in the answer to this question the role that excessive responsibility plays in guilt, I do wish to stress that it is not taking excessive responsibility on its own that leads to guilt. Rather it is the demand that you absolutely must do the right thing (or absolutely must not do the wrong thing) in areas in which you consider yourself to be responsible. Indeed, I believe that once you hold a set of demands, which is at the core of the guilt experience, this philosophy leads you to take far more responsibility than is warranted. As I will show later in this book, if you want to reduce your sense of responsibility to human limits, and come to an objective appraisal of the other factors impinging on a negative event, it is important that you first work to give up your demanding philosophy about your moral code violations and the harm you inflict on others. It is difficult to be objective about responsibility when you are feeling very guilty!

3

Other People and
Guilt Feelings

In this chapter, I look at the relationship between guilt and other people in your life. I consider the role that blame and responsibility play in guilt and the fact that you may have trouble admitting your 'sins'. I also make the important point that other people do not make you feel guilty – only you can do that!

From what you have said, it follows that guilt increases the chances of our violating our moral codes and hurting other people. I have always thought that guilt was meant to prevent us from doing these things. Can you clarify?

When you are feeling guilty about violating a moral code, for example, you are demanding that you absolutely should not have done this and that you are a bad person for so doing. As such, you become preoccupied with your own badness. This guilty pre-occupation then makes it much harder for you to stand back and to consider the reasons why you may have violated your moral code in the first place. It also makes it harder for you to consider the steps you need to take to prevent yourself from violating your moral code again. Since you have failed to learn anything about why you might have acted as you did and what you can do in the future to prevent this, you are more likely to violate the same code again in the future than you would be if you experienced constructive remorse. When you are feeling remorseful, but not guilty, about violating your moral code, this feeling alerts you to the need to address the issue. You are then increasingly likely to stand back and reflect in a reasoned way about why you violated

31

your code in the first place and what you can do differently in the future to prevent this happening again.

In short, then, guilt interferes both with your understanding your wrongdoing and with your learning from your mistakes. In contrast, remorse aids your understanding of why you acted the way you did and helps you to think more objectively about what you need to do differently in the face of the same set of circumstances.

Let me also answer this question in a slightly different way. When you are experiencing guilt you will recall that one of your attitudes is that you are a bad person for violating your moral code. Since you are defining yourself as a bad person rather than a fallible human being who has committed a bad act, you are making a statement about your core identity. You literally believe, at this time, that you are bad through and through for acting in a bad manner. Let me ask you, what kind of behaviour does a bad person do? The answer is he or she acts badly. Therefore, since you are a bad person in your own eyes, this statement about your identity makes it more likely that you will violate your code in the future and less likely that you will act in a more ethical way when faced with the same set of circumstances.

However, when you accept yourself as a fallible human being and you take responsibility for acting badly, this more compassionate statement about your core identity means that you can improve in the future. Being a fallible human being – which means that you have the capacity to act both well and badly – implies that you can learn from the experience and act more ethically in future. When you consider yourself a bad person, you literally doom yourself to acting badly in the future. There is literally no way that a bad person can act ethically.

We can apply this analysis to an experience that is unfortunately common to most of us: gluttony.

Jill had been on a diet for two weeks and had successfully adhered to it. Then she learned some upsetting news about one of her close friends and rather than deal with her emotional upset, she did what she normally does and turned to food for short-term comfort. Observing that she had broken her diet and acted in what she considered to be a gluttonous manner, Jill experienced guilt about this violation. She believed that she absolutely should not have broken her diet and acted in a gluttonous manner, and that she was a wicked person for doing so. This feeling of guilt and the related identity that she constructed for herself, namely that she was wicked, led her to eat even more gluttonously than before. Why? First, because she increased her dysphoria which, given her tendency to cope with upsetting feelings through eating, led her to eat even more in a futile attempt to get rid of her distress. Second, since she believed that she was a wicked person for acting in this gluttonous manner, this belief about her core identity, namely her badness, led to a self-fulfilling prophecy. Since she was bad she continued to act badly and in this example eat even more gluttonously than before.

If Jill had been able to experience constructive remorse about her original violation of her diet instead of guilt, she could have spared herself much needless emotional pain and learnt from the experience. If she believed that, while it was undesirable for her to break her diet, there was no law of the universe that decreed that she must not do so, the resulting constructive feelings of remorse that she would have experienced would have motivated her to ask herself the question: 'Why did I eat so much when I was experiencing emotional upset?' This would have encouraged her to think about her self-defeating ways of handling emotional upsets and would have motivated her to look for more helpful alternatives in dealing with her distress. Second, her more healthy attitude that she was a fallible human being for breaking her diet rather than a wicked person would have inspired hope that she could respond to emotional upset in more productive and less 'wicked' ways.

Let me apply this analysis to existential guilt (see p. 2). You will remember that existential guilt stems from a rigid attitude about yourself, namely that you are bad through and through no matter what you do. Since you consider yourself bad through and through and therefore literally irredeemable, this judgemental, inflexible attitude about yourself literally increases the chances of your acting in ways which are consistent with your attitude towards yourself. In other words, you will increase the chances of acting unethically in the future. If you are a bad person through and through and that is in your nature, you will continue to act badly because that is what bad people do.

While we are on the subject, let me deal with another question that people raise which is relevant to this issue. If you discourage people from feeling guilty do you encourage them to act psychopathically? My answer is a resounding *No!* Psychopaths not only refrain from blaming themselves, they also do not acknowledge responsibility for breaking moral codes or hurting other people. Even if they do acknowledge responsibility for doing these things they literally do not consider that they have acted badly. They have, as the term psychopath implies, no conscience. When you experience constructive remorse, remember, it is important that while you are not blaming yourself for acting badly, you are (1) acknowledging responsibility for your behaviour, and (2) recognizing that you have either violated a moral code, failed to live up to some ethical principle or hurt somebody by the consequences of your actions. So I do not believe that I am encouraging people to become psychopaths by suggesting that they experience constructive remorse rather than guilt; rather I am encouraging them to act ethically while refraining from unethically damning themselves.

Does guilt and the self-blame that is a part of it also make us more likely to blame other people?

In my experience, yes. As I discussed earlier, most forms of guilt stem from the interpretation that you have done wrong, failed to adhere to some ethical principle or have 'hurt' others. You then demand that you absolutely should not have acted in the way that you did or that you absolutely should have done what you didn't do and then you blame yourself and regard yourself as something of a bad, rotten or wicked person for your wrongdoing. Since self-blame is a form of anger towards yourself, it is frequently related to anger towards other people. Thus, when you consider that another person has broken a moral code, failed to live up to an important ethical principle, or has hurt another person, you not only consider that they have done the wrong thing, for example, but you also bring your demanding, condemning attitude to the situation. Thus you believe that the other person absolutely should not have done what she did and that she is a rotten individual for doing so who deserves to be punished for her wrongdoing.

The healthy alternative to blaming others is to accept them as fallible human beings, while holding them responsible for their actions. Thus when you observe that somebody has broken a moral code, a healthy attitude towards this situation is to hold her responsible for her bad behaviour, but to recognize that she is not a bad person for so doing. Rather, she is a fallible human being who did the wrong thing. In this way you can help the person to take responsibility for her actions without blaming her for them. If you approach the other person from a blaming position then you decrease the chances that she will take responsibility for and learn from her actions, and increase the probability that she will either blame herself for her wrongdoing on the one hand, or deny that she has acted wrongly, or make excuses for her wrongful behaviour, on the other.

One way of ridding yourself of your blaming attitude towards others when they act wrongfully is to work towards minimizing your guilt-creating philosophy and replacing it with a remorse-creating philosophy. This, as you will now realize, involves accepting yourself for your own wrongful behaviour while taking full responsibility for what you have done. The more you are able to accept yourself for your good and bad points, the more you will accept others for theirs and the less you will blame them for their 'sins'.

In addition to increasing the chances that you will blame others for their sins, guilty self-blame also has a number of other negative results. First, it increases your dependency on external authorities and interferes with your ability to think for yourself. You are more likely to accept uncritically standards that have been passed down from generation to generation that may no longer be applicable to modern-day living. Your rigidity – namely your absolute demand that you must not act badly or must act well – leads you to live in a black-and-white world where nuances and subtleties do not exist. Since your thinking is black and white, you may wrongly conclude that you are totally responsible for an event which has followed on from your behaviour or that you are not at all responsible for it. By contrast, flexible thinking – which is closely related to the idea that it would be preferable not to act badly, but there's no law of the universe that says you absolutely must not do so – allows you to stand back and think more clearly about how much responsibility you can realistically assume for the consequences of your actions.

Second, guilt tends to lead to over-dependency on others and, therefore, to a situation where you sacrifice yourself so that others may pursue their interests. While it is healthy to put others first some of the time, to sacrifice yourself continually so that others achieve their goals is bound to lead to a frustrating life unless you truly derive joy from continually putting other people first. This type of guilt is mainly related to the ideas that you absolutely must not hurt other people's feelings and that you are a bad person if you do. Since you are horrified at the thought of 'hurting' other people, you consistently strive to ensure that nobody experiences hurtful feelings as a result of your behaviour. This means that you must continually put other people first and help them to meet their desires. Thereby, you become dependent on their having good feelings towards you or at the very least on their not feeling negative towards you. In this way, guilt leads to self-sacrifice and dependency on others.

Third, a guilt-creating, self-blaming philosophy leads you to dwell on your past wrongdoings rather than to learn from your past mistakes and apply such learning to the present and future. If you experience guilt about the past, you continually believe that you absolutely should not have acted in the way that you did.

A moment's reflection will lead you to realize that this is a ridiculous philosophy because what you are in effect saying is this: first, you recognize that you acted badly and that this actually happened. Therefore it constituted reality at that time. Second, you demand that reality absolutely should not be reality! If it was reality, it should have existed because all the conditions were in place for it to have existed. So, rather than demand that the conditions absolutely should have been different, you can help yourself much more effectively by acknowledging that all the conditions were in place for you to act as you did.

Having done this you could then ask yourself several questions:

- Can I understand why I acted as I did?
- Can I understand what was going through my mind at the time that led me to act in the way that I did?
- Can I change such thinking so I can act more responsibly in the future?
- What can I learn from this experience to minimize such wrongful behaviour in the future?

It is very difficult to engage in such healthy problem-solving behaviour when you are condemning yourself for doing what you believe you absolutely should not have done.

Fourth, guilt-creating self-blame tends to increase your anxiety lest you act in a similar wrongful way in the future. Such anxiety once again tends to interfere with your ability to think clearly and thereby paradoxically increases the chances that you may act wrongfully in the future. Since you are not processing information in a constructive way, you fail to see the relationship between past and potential wrongful behaviour with the result that you don't learn from the past and fail to prevent your wrongful behaviour in the future. As I often say to my clients, the prototype of anxiety is the headless chicken. How clearly do headless chickens think when they are frantically dashing hither and thither in search of they know not what?

While self-blame may occasionally help you to act more

constructively in the future, by far the most frequent consequences of self-blame are self-defeating negative ones as I have shown in the answer to your question.

Why do some people have trouble admitting to themselves and others that they have done something wrong?

The basic answer to this is that by denying your wrongdoing, you protect yourself from guilt. If you did admit to yourself and other people that you were responsible for a wrongdoing, you would severely condemn yourself for this wrongdoing. It is to protect yourself from self-condemning guilt that you adopt a variety of ways of denying responsibility.

One of the major ways of denying that you have committed some wrongdoing is to blame another person. This tactic occurs in the Bible when Adam and Eve ate from the tree of knowledge. Adam blamed Eve for giving him the apple; in turn, Eve blamed the serpent. Both were operating from the idea, 'I didn't do it, it was somebody else'. Indeed young children spontaneously use this tactic when they are caught doing something wrong. They immediately deny that they committed the act and put the blame on somebody else. All parents are familiar with this phenomenon and some may be driven to exasperation by children who keep blaming others for their own wrongdoings.

Two common tactics to protect yourself from guilt involve your denying that your act was indeed wrong and making excuses for your wrongdoing. An example of the latter is when you explain away your wrongdoing by attributing your behaviour to tiredness or to some strange external feeling outside of yourself: 'It just came over me.'

You may employ a variety of defence mechanisms, the purpose of which is to defend yourself against guilt. These are generally outside your awareness, so you will have to look for them and ask yourself honestly if you are using one or more of them. A common defence mechanism is projection, where you project your feelings onto another person.

Jim, a very upright, middle-aged married man, experienced lustful feelings towards his secretary although he did not allow himself to acknowledge this, since doing so would lead him to condemn himself for the sin of lust. Instead, he projected his lustful feelings onto his wife of whom he became suspicious, accusing her of having lustful feelings towards other men.

Reaction formation is another defence mechanism, albeit less commonly employed, which protects you from guilt. In reaction formation, you develop feelings opposite to those you are really experiencing.

Susan had angry feelings towards her child and did not recognize this because, again, she would condemn herself if she did so. To compensate, she became over-protective of her child. This over-protection convinces her that she is not the kind of person to harbour destructive thoughts and urges towards her child. Her over-protection is a reaction against her destructive urges.

Obsessive-compulsion is a commonly used defence mechanism to ward off guilt which I discussed earlier (see pp. 24–7). If you are in the habit of compulsively checking a potentially harmful aspect of your home environment (especially where gas and electricity are involved), you do so in order to be absolutely certain that no possible harm will result from your failure to make your environment completely safe. If any harm did result, no matter how slight, you would feel guilty. Thus, your compulsion helps you to avoid guilt. In addition, you may have developed compulsive work habits to ward off self-accusations of laziness. Here you would condemn yourself mercilessly for being lazy and experience guilt as a result. In the circumstances, your workaholism protects you from guilt.

Other defence mechanisms include intellectualization, withdrawal and sublimation. In intellectualization, you cut yourself off from most or all of your feelings so that you do not experience guilt over some wrongdoing. In withdrawal, you do not take any risks so that you are certain that you have not done anything wrong. Finally, as Sigmund Freud noted, people often sublimate their aggressive impulses into acceptable forms of behaviour. Thus, if you feel aggressive you may take up boxing or rugby as a legitimate expression of your aggressiveness. You may do this because if you expressed your aggressiveness in less legitimate ways, you would feel guilty about such expression.

To summarize, human beings are quite creative at defending themselves against guilt. You do so because you have the following guilt-creating philosophies which I have described earlier in this book:

- 'I absolutely must not do anything wrong.'
- 'I absolutely must live up to my moral code.'
- 'I must not harm anyone.'
- 'I am a bad person if I fail to live up to my demands.'

However, if you develop a more healthy philosophy leading to constructive remorse:

- you will not need to employ defence mechanisms;
- you will be more able to take and admit responsibility for your wrongdoings;
- you will learn from your errors and make appropriate amends.

The other part of your question concerns why you might find it difficult to admit your wrongdoings to other people. In addition to the reasons discussed above, namely that you would condemn yourself if you did admit your wrongdoings to another person, there are a variety of other reasons why you may not admit responsibility for your sins in public. The first reason is your prediction that other people will condemn you if they learn of your wrongdoings. Part of this fear is a legitimate one in the sense that some people would blame you if you did admit your sins to them. However, other people would take a more compassionate, understanding approach if you admitted your wrongdoing publicly. The fear that you will be condemned and blamed by other people stems in large part from the attitude that you are a bad person for committing the wrongdoing and deserve to be punished for it.

This fear of punishment also lies behind the other main reason why you may not publicly acknowledge wrongful behaviour. Here, you fear that if you were to do so then other people would exact retribution from you, either by taking 'an eye for an eye' or by ensuring that you fail to achieve a desired goal.

Sam, a business executive, destroyed some company documents while in an angry phase of a grief reaction following his mother's death. Sam feared that if he admitted to his wrongdoing other people would not understand and would ensure that he would either be dismissed from the company or be demoted. He severely condemned himself for his behaviour and did not make allowances for it. He believed that no matter how angry he was or how much he grieved for the loss of his mother, he absolutely shouldn't have acted in the way that he did. Sam did not own up to his behaviour but a company investigation discovered that he was responsible for destroying the documents. To his amazement, Sam's bosses took quite a compassionate, understanding view of this and assured him that it would not affect his future career. Indeed, one of his bosses said to him, 'Sam, I know exactly what you must have gone through because I lost my own father two years ago and I went through an angry phase then as well.' Sam's failure to empathize with his own behaviour blinded him to the fact that other people might take an empathic, compassionate view when they learned of his wrongdoing.

Since your judgement about the wisdom of publicly owning up to a wrongdoing is coloured by your guilt-creating beliefs, it is important for you first to accept yourself for your wrongdoing before asking yourself the question, 'Is it wise for me to disclose my behaviour to others, knowing what I know about them?' In closing, I do want to stress, however, that some people *will* blame you if they find out about your wrongful behaviour and may well seek to exact retribution from you; so do not disclose your wrongful behaviour in a cavalier, indiscriminate fashion. Rather, first accept yourself and then consider the *likely* consequences of your public disclosure, before you decide on a course of action.

A lot of people I know would feel guilty if they hurt other people's feelings, so they keep their own feelings to themselves. What should they do?

Guilt about hurting other people's feelings is unfortunately quite common. It is a major factor in stopping people from honestly expressing their feelings and leads people to subordinate their own desires to those of others.

In reality, you cannot hurt other people's feelings even if you say something very rude or highly critical to them. This is because your rude and critical behaviour serves as a stimulus for their own upset-creating beliefs which in turn lead them to feel distressed and disturbed about what you have said. Unfortunately, many people who hear this think that I am advocating an 'anything goes' approach and that I am absolving people from their responsibility for choosing how they say things to another person. Let me make it perfectly clear: I am not advocating this; I am a firm advocate of respectful communication to other people and encourage you to take full responsibility concerning what you say and how you say it.

Having noted that it is psychologically impossible for you directly to hurt another person's feelings, let's leave that to one side for the moment and assume that you can indeed hurt his or her feelings. Should you feel guilty about this? As I've shown throughout this book, my answer is a resounding *No*. Why? Suppose you have said something or done something which can be objectively regarded as critical, harsh and uncaring. I strongly urge you to accept responsibility for your behaviour and to acknowledge your wrongdoing. Further, since I am now assuming that you can hurt another person's feelings, I encourage you to take responsibility for this too. However, you only feel guilty about this if you demand that you absolutely should not have done what you did and that you are a bad person for (i) your actions, and (ii) upsetting the other person's feelings. If you want to refrain from feeling guilty then you need to show yourself that while you have done the wrong thing, there is no reason why you absolutely should not have committed the wrongdoing and that you are a fallible human being for so doing. This attitude will lead you to feel healthily remorseful which will in turn encourage you to reflect on your words and behaviour to ascertain why you said and acted as you did, and what you can learn from the experience to minimize future wrongdoings. In addition, since you acknowledge that you have acted in an uncaring and hurtful manner, your non-self-blaming attitude will encourage you to try to make amends to the other person, to seek a reconciliation if this is possible.

Now, let's assume that you have not yet decided to voice your critical feelings or act in a way which may lead the other person to be hurt or distressed. What can you do in this situation? First, think clearly about how you can express yourself as caringly and respectfully as possible, but without backing down from what you want to say. Second, imagine that the other person's feelings will be hurt, even by your considered words, and show yourself that it is healthy to be remorseful about this. Watch for your tendency to make yourself guilty, as you do when you think that you are a bad person who absolutely should not have hurt the other person's feelings. Work to give up this demand and to accept yourself as a fallible human being who has said something about which the other person has disturbed him- or herself. Having done this, realize that you have a choice whether you speak up or not. If you decide to speak up, realize that this may be the best course of action for you *in the long run*, even though the other person's feelings may be hurt *in the short run*. If you choose unselfishly to look after your own interests, the grim reality is that this sometimes means others close to you will be hurt and upset. I stress the phrase 'unselfishly look after your own interests' because too many people consider putting their own interests first to be selfish. Strictly speaking, selfish means (a) not caring *at all* about another person's feelings, and (b) *only* looking out for yourself. The idea that you can unselfishly look after your own interests and be sad and remorseful when this means that other people are hurt by what you say is based on a philosophy of enlightened self-interest.

Brenda has kindly allowed me to tell her story, although to respect her confidentiality I have changed any identifying material. When she was in her teens, Brenda met a young man and became engaged to him, even though she had doubts about their relationship right from the start. However, her father, whom she loved dearly, got on famously with her fiancé and was delighted that they were to be married. However, Brenda harboured her doubts right up to the week before the wedding. She tentatively tried to explain how she felt to her father, but backed off immediately when he began to become upset. How can I not go through with the wedding, she thought, when this would hurt my father so much? Consequently, she went through with the marriage which was unhappy right from the beginning.

Brenda remained in the relationship for far more years than was healthy for her because she was scared of the impact that the breakup of the marriage would have on her father: she still thought he would be terribly upset if they split up. When her father died she felt more able to think of ending the relationship, but was faced with the knowledge that her husband would then be terribly upset. So she remained in the marriage in a futile attempt to patch things up. To cope with her emotional pain, Brenda took to alcohol. Even this did not work and eventually she plucked up the courage to end the marriage. Predictably, her husband was very hurt and upset and Brenda made herself very guilty about upsetting his feelings. She intensified her drinking habits to the point where she needed professional help for her problem drinking.

Fortunately, the story has a happy ending. Brenda

discovered the principles of rational-emotive behaviour therapy on which this book is based and helped herself to rid herself of her guilt. She did this by acknowledging that she was sad and remorseful if other people were hurt by her actions, but that this was an unfortunate fact of life. She further recognized that if she did not put herself first, nobody else would. Brenda laments the wasted years, and wishes that she knew then how she needlessly made herself feel guilty about upsetting her father in the first place and her husband in the second place. I hope you can see from Brenda's story how self-defeating it is to keep your doubts and reservations to yourself about relationships, rather than hurt other people's feelings.

In summary, acknowledge that hurting people's feelings is an unfortunate fact of life since other people frequently have different desires from yours. Adopt the position of enlightened self-interest (not selfishness!) and put your own important desires first, while being respectful and mindful of other people's desires. Recognize that if you put other people first on issues which are significant to you, you are putting them first, they are putting themselves first and nobody is putting you first! Recognize too that when other people's feelings are hurt, assuming that you have communicated your feelings in a direct yet respectful way, they mainly hurt themselves about what you have said. Even when you overreact and say things which would hurt most people, accept yourself for making this error and learn from it. As Brenda's case shows, it is better to take the risk to express yourself, even if this means hurting another person's feelings, rather than live a life where you are significantly unhappy in order to protect your loved ones from temporary hurt feelings.

But surely if you've done something bad and another person is involved, then you are responsible for the actions of that other person and you should feel guilty, shouldn't you?

My answer to this one, again, is a resounding *No*. Tony Gough, in his very interesting book on guilt, responsibility and blame, *Don't Blame Me*, describes a situation where a wife, on discovering her husband's affair, takes herself off in her car with her child and drives over a cliff, killing them both. Gough asks who is to blame for this tragedy. He notes, correctly in my view, that the husband is responsible for having the affair, knowing that if it is discovered it would certainly have an adverse effect on his wife. The other woman, too, also has responsibility for having an affair with a married man. However, Gough asks, doesn't the wife have most of the responsibility for killing herself and their child? He points out that there are numerous things she could have done instead of taking such drastic action. First of all, she could have accepted the affair with good grace and continued the marriage, either allowing the affair to go on or insisting that her husband give up his mistress. She could have, without distress, sued for divorce. She could have made herself angry about the affair and resolved to get as much compensation as possible from her husband in a divorce action. As Gough notes, she could have killed the mistress, killed her husband, or just killed herself without killing the child.

Please note that I am not advocating that anybody be blamed for this tragedy but that all take responsibility for what they are in fact responsible for. The husband should take responsibility for the part his affair played in his wife's decision to kill herself and the child, while not taking responsibility for her decision to do so. Regretfully, her drastic decision can only be her responsibility. Now it may be said that she acted in the way she did because she was very emotionally disturbed by discovering her husband's affair. However, this does not mean that her husband should take responsibility for her actions since he was not the one who drove the car over the cliff with his wife and child in it.

However, what if the husband in this case was directly responsible for his wife and child's death? Surely he should feel guilty about this? My answer is that he should definitely feel remorseful, but he doesn't need to damn himself for his actions. Blaming or damning yourself for committing an extremely serious wrongdoing is counter-productive since it stops you from learning from what you have done, so that you cannot take appropriate action to minimize its happening again.

Let's take the case of Nathan Leopold who, with another man, killed a young boy for a thrill. This North American case, which happened in the 1920s, was labelled at the time the crime of the century. Should Nathan Leopold have felt very guilty about his crime (rather than healthily remorseful) by damning himself and considering himself an evil person? If he had done so, he would have not been able to do what he did after he was released from prison many years later. On his release, Nathan Leopold was a changed individual. He became a social worker, he got married and spent the rest of his life doing very good works. My point is this: if Nathan Leopold had damned himself and considered himself to be an evil person, he would have not been able to reform himself. How can an evil person be reformed since his very nature is evil? Let me stress again that I am not absolving people like Nathan Leopold from responsibility for their actions. Rather I am suggesting that they acknowledge their crimes and accept themselves for their actions. In this way they can learn from their gross misdeeds, reform themselves, pay their dues to society and live as healthily as possible in the future.

In summary, take responsibility for your own actions, show yourself how they may have contributed to another person's actions, but do not take responsibility for what that other person has done. Even if you are directly responsible for another person's actions, feel healthily remorseful about this rather than unhealthily guilty. By this I mean that you need to accept responsibility for what you've done, accept yourself for your misdeeds, learn from the experience, pay the penalty and get on with your life.

Other people make me feel guilty. How can I stop them?

The first important point to realize is that other people cannot make you feel guilty. As I have shown throughout this book, guilt stems from the following guilt-creating philosophy: 'I must do the right thing (or not do the wrong thing), and I am a bad person if I fail to do the right thing (or do the wrong thing).' Guilt also stems from the philosophy, 'I absolutely must not hurt another person's feelings and I am a bad person if I do.' These forms of guilt are called episodic guilt because they are related to specific episodes. Finally, there is existential guilt which stems from an enduring philosophy: 'I am bad through and through no matter what I do.' So when you say that other people make you feel guilty, you are implying that they have direct control over your feelings. This is not the case since your feelings stem largely from your attitudes about yourself, other people and the world. This is a very important point to remember when other people try to make you feel guilty.

Let me put this in a slightly different way. Let us suppose that your mother says to you, 'If you don't do this for me, then you don't love me and you are a bad person.' One way of looking at this statement is to say that it constitutes an invitation from your mother. Your mother is stating that she thinks you are a bad person if you don't do something for her and she is inviting you to define yourself as a bad person if you fail to do her bidding. As with any invitation, this can be accepted or declined. Can you see the difference between accepting your mother's invitation: 'Yes mother, I am a bad person if I do not do this for you', and rejecting the invitation: 'No mother, I am not a bad person even though I'm not doing this for you'? Your guilt therefore stems not from what your mother says to you, but from your acceptance of her invitation which you then apply to yourself: 'I am a bad person if I fail to help my mother.'

People who successfully manipulate you into feeling guilty play on your overdeveloped tendency to accept responsibility for their happiness. That is, you have a philosophy which states: 'I am responsible for the well-being and happiness of people significant to me. If these people are unhappy, I caused their unhappiness and I am a bad person for causing it.' As I have already mentioned, it is important to take responsibility for your own behaviour. If you decide not to do something for a person

48

who is trying to make you feel guilty, take responsibility for how you communicate your unwillingness. If you do this with hostility you need to take responsibility for your hostile behaviour, recognize that this has largely contributed to, but still by no means caused the other person's unhappiness, and accept yourself for your hostile behaviour. This will help you learn what led you to be hostile so that you can deal with a similar future situation in a more helpful fashion. However, if you communicate your unwillingness in a polite manner and the other person is unhappy about this, then it is important that you allow the other person to take responsibility for his or her own unhappy feelings.

When other people try to make you feel guilty, recognize that they are doing this in order to control your behaviour. Basically, the other person either wants you to do something that she would feel pleased with or does not want you to do something that she would be displeased with. She therefore implies (a) that you are a bad person for not complying with her wishes, and (b) that you are responsible for how she feels. This can be communicated in a direct manner as when your father says to you 'Your mother has had a nervous breakdown worrying about you.' Here the message is clearly: you were responsible for your mother's breakdown. Or it can be done in a more subtle manner as when your mother says, 'Don't worry about me dear, I'll be all right.' The covert message here is, 'I'm not all right and it is all your fault.' It is important that you:

- realize the controlling, manipulative intent behind such messages;
- accept the other person for her controlling behaviour;
- realize that you do not have to do what she wants;
- remind yourself that you do not have to assume responsibility for the other person's happiness.

Manipulation through guilt commonly occurs when somebody says to you 'If you loved me, you wouldn't do that.' Here the implication is that if you continue to act in the way to which the other person objects, you do not love him. Realize clearly that you can continue to act in the way that the other person dislikes *and* you can still love him. The former does not preclude the latter.

As Vernon Coleman notes in his book *How to Stop Feeling Guilty* (Sheldon Press, 1982), much advertising plays on your tendency to be easily manipulated by guilt. A well-known advertisement begins 'Do you love someone enough to . . .' Here, the implication is that if you do not buy their product, this means that you do not love the person concerned and therefore you are something of a bad person. My point is that you can still love someone and not buy the product!

Manipulation by guilt, as a means of social control, most frequently occurs in over-involved families and closely-knit social groups. In addition to the idea that your behaviour can be controlled by others' implying that you do not love them if you continue to act in a certain way, accusations of bringing shame upon the family or social group is also designed to encourage you to feel guilty. Here the message is that if you act in a certain way, this will lead your family, for example, to be shamed in the eyes of others, you are responsible for this and are a bad person as a result. Only take responsibility for what you are responsible for. Even if you are responsible for bringing shame on your family, this is a matter of deep remorse rather than for self-condemning guilt. However, in most instances, your actions will not directly cause shame to come on your family since shame is based on an attitude for which the holder of the attitude is responsible. Thus, do not allow yourself to be manipulated by other people implying that you do not love them or that you will bring shame on them, although you may wish to take this into consideration when you decide whether or not to act in a certain way.

Let me give a personal example to demonstrate how I did not allow myself to be manipulated by my family's attempts to make me feel guilty. In my late teens I decided to change my name from David Denbin to Windy Dryden. I chose Windy because it was a nickname that I was given at a time when I played the saxophone and because I adopted it during a six-month stay in a kibbutz. Furthermore, I liked the name. I decided to change the name from Denbin to Dryden because I had a very bad stammer and found Denbin very difficult to pronounce without stammering. I thus decided that since it was my name I would choose to change it in the way that suited me. When I announced this intention to my family they were, understandably, quite upset. They tried to dissuade me from changing my name by accusing me, first, of being selfish; second, of not loving them; and third, of ending at one fell swoop the Denbin name.

As you can see, I still decided to change my name. How did I resist such pressure? I did so because I did not accept their definition that I was acting selfishly. I considered that I was acting according to the philosophy of enlightened self-interest, in which I put my interests first while at the same time feeling concerned about the distress that they would experience. However, I did not allow their distress to dictate my decision. I did not accept my parents' viewpoint that I did not love them, because I knew that I did, and that whether I changed my name or not had no bearing on my degree of love for them. The fact that I would be bringing the family name to an end did concern me, but on balance I decided to change it since (a) I did not like the name, and (b) I was fed up sounding like a machine gun as I stammered my way through my surname. My parents still, over twenty years later, call me David, not Windy, and I do not object to this. We still love one another and while they are still regretful about my decision, it has not affected our relationship when viewed from a long-term perspective.

Let me close this section by making the following statement. If you believe that others make you feel guilty, you are not taking responsibility for what you can control, namely your own feelings, and are taking responsibility for what you cannot control, namely their feelings!

Why do I feel guilty when I don't return a favour?

The reason that you feel guilty about not returning a favour is that you consider that you are obliged to return the favour, that is, you believe that you *have to* reciprocate and that you are a selfish, ungrateful person if you do not. Some people deliberately use this feeling of obligation as a ploy to manipulate others. Thus, they will do a favour for you in order to have you do a favour for them later. Salesmen use this tactic with a high level of skill. I know of one drug salesman who makes an appointment to see a family doctor and spends some time speaking to the receptionist a week before the appointment in order to ascertain the doctor's hobbies. For example, if a doctor likes playing golf, the salesman will turn up with a gift of a new putter and only later ask the doctor to use his company's product. Nine times out of ten the doctor promises to use the drug because she would feel guilty about refusing. How can the doctor refuse to use the product and not feel guilty? First, she needs to recognize that one act, namely accepting the gift, has no bearing on the other act, namely, agreeing to use the drug. Even if she makes this connection, in order to refuse, the doctor needs to believe: 'While I would like to reciprocate, I don't have to do so and certainly not by promising to use the drugs that are produced by the salesman's company. I will choose to use the drugs which are in the best interests of my patients, rather than to tie myself into an obligation which does not exist unless I deem it to exist. I regret not being able to return the favour, and I'm not an ungrateful, selfish and something of a bad person for my refusal.'

Shop assistants use a similar tactic. They spend a lot of time with you helping you to choose a product in which you have shown an interest. They do so in order that you will feel guilty about wasting their time. As I have shown many of my clients over the years, shop assistants will receive their salary whether or not you buy a product you do not want. In fact, it is part of their job to have their time wasted. However, even if you are responsible for wasting their time, and let's suppose that that is an unfortunate wrongdoing, how does it therefore follow that you are a bad person for committing such a wrongdoing? The answer is that it does not follow. It is an unwarranted conclusion. You have a human right to do the wrong thing, and refrain from buying the product, no matter how much of the shop assistant's time you waste. Please note, however, that I am not advocating the deliberate misuse of shop assistants' time. What I am advocating is that if you do have an interest in the product, you do not have to buy it just because you have spent time with somebody who has shown you care and attention.

If you want to learn more about being able to say no without making yourself feel guilty, read Manuel J. Smith's book, *When I Say No, I Feel Guilty* (Bantam, 1975). This book is a classic in the field of assertiveness training and I strongly recommend it.

4

Guilt and Related Problems

Here, I consider how guilt relates to other problems such as anger and low-frustration tolerance. I make the important distinction between enlightened self-interest, selfishness and selflessness, consider the protective and phoney aspects of guilt and distinguish between shame and guilt, two emotions which are often confused.

How does guilt relate to other emotional or behavioural problems that I may have?

There are two psychological problems about which you may especially make yourself guilty. The first is anger – either when you experience it or, more typically, when you express it in damaging ways. An example of guilt over expressed anger can be illustrated in the case of Robert.

Robert was a hard-working employee who applied for promotion at his job and was refused it. He made himself angry about this not only because he considered that his boss was unfair for denying him promotion which he thought he fully deserved, but mainly because he further believed that his boss should have granted him his just deserts. Robert was so angry that he went into his boss's office and yelled at him in a fit of rage. Afterwards he became very guilty because he believed that he was wrong to yell at his boss in the way that he did, and that he absolutely shouldn't have yelled at him, and that he was a bad person for doing so.

Recall that guilt prevents you from understanding and learning from your errors. So instead of reflecting on his anger and finding out what brought it about (namely his angercreating philosophy) Robert's guilt led him to become preoccupied with his own sense of wickedness, which in turn led him in an inappropriate manner to beg his boss to forgive him. In order for Robert to feel constructively remorseful, instead of guilty, he needed to challenge his belief that he absolutely should not have acted in the way that he did and that he was a bad person for doing so. Having accepted himself for his error, he could have then apologized to his boss in an adult fashion. He could also have identified his anger-creating philosophy, which he could then have challenged by giving up his demand that his boss absolutely should have treated him fairly.

Another example of the role that guilt plays in anger and other problems can be seen in the case of Sarah.

Sarah was aware that she did not meet all of her children's needs. She believed that she absolutely should meet their needs and that she was a bad person for not doing so. She thus felt guilty. However, she was also aware that she found her children very demanding and believed that they absolutely should not be so demanding of her time and attention. This led her to feel resentful towards her children. She then focused on her feelings of resentment and believed that she absolutely should not experience such feelings for her children, a demand that led her to feel more guilt. In this way Sarah trapped herself in what I call the guilt-resentment-guilt trap. Caught in this trap, she was unable to challenge her demands towards herself and towards her children. In order to extricate herself from this trap, Sarah would need to challenge the idea that she had to meet all of her children's needs and that she must not feel resentment towards them. She would also have to challenge her demand that they must not be so needy. If she could challenge these demands, then she would feel remorseful about not meeting their needs and sorry that she experienced resentment towards them. She would also feel annoyed that they are so needy. Experiencing these more constructive negative emotions would help her to set healthy boundaries, both for herself and her children, so that she could respond more appropriately to their demanding behaviour. Indeed, once she challenged her resentment-creating and guilt-creating philosophies, she was able to see that her children were so demanding because she had withdrawn from them in her attempt to cope with her failure to meet their needs. This helped her to become more involved with them, with the result that they became less demanding.

We also make ourselves guilty when we act according to our philosophy of low frustration tolerance. A typical example of this is when we break diets.

Mary successfully adhered to her diet for a month. Then she became angry towards her children's nanny, felt ashamed of her angry feelings and in a desperate attempt to cope with her shame, turned to food. Realizing that she had broken her diet, she made herself feel guilty about her gluttonous behaviour. This guilt increased her diet-breaking behaviour and discouraged her from resuming her diet. During counselling, Mary was helped to accept herself for her angry feelings towards her children's nanny. She was shown that her failure to cope with her feelings of shame encouraged her to break her diet. She was then helped to give up her demand that she absolutely should not have acted in a gluttonous way and this helped her to resume her diet.

Mary's example shows quite clearly that when you have difficulty in coping with frustrating situations because of your philosophy of low-frustration tolerance (e.g. I can't stand this frustration and I have to get rid of it immediately), you tend to act in an uncontrolled manner. If you then make yourself guilty about your uncontrolled behaviour, this guilt tends to increase your sense of being out of control and you act accordingly.

In all these examples, that is, guilt about anger, shame and uncontrolled behaviour, your feelings of guilt tend to exacerbate your problems rather than ameliorate them. In contrast, when you successfully challenge your guilt-creating philosophies, and experience constructive remorse about your problems, you help yourself to understand why you acted as you did in the first place. You can then learn to challenge the demands that underpin those problems and, in doing so, you increase your chances of coping with them.

Does guilt stop us from putting ourselves first?

Let me answer this important question by distinguishing between three different philosophies. The most healthy of these philosophies is called enlightened self-interest. In enlightened self-interest you care both for yourself and for those who are closest to you. Your basic standpoint is that unless you look after your own interests, it is unlikely that any other individual will put you first, unless they are doing so for disturbed reasons. Putting yourself first does not mean, as I shall stress, being selfish. It means that you are aware of what is important to you in life and that you strive to achieve this, while being mindful that other people close to you also have their own interests and that you will help them pursue these, as long as doing so does not significantly interfere with your own healthy interests. Enlightened self-interest is a flexible position since it means that at times you will put other people's interests above your own when their interests are significantly important to them and when your interests are less important to you. However, you will not generally allow yourself to put other people's significant interests before your own significant interests.

The second basic philosophy that I wish to discuss is selfishness. My definition of selfishness is a consistent, even dogmatic pursuit of your own interests while being unconcerned with the interests and feelings of others. Selfishness means that you are *only* concerned with yourself and *un*concerned with others. As a result, you make little or no attempt to help other people achieve what is important to them, if that means doing without what is important to you, no matter how minor your own interests are.

It is unfortunate that enlightened self-interest is often labelled selfishness because, as you can see, they are very different philosophies. Selfishness is based on your preoccupation with yourself and lack of interest in others, while enlightened self-interest is based on a concern with both yourself and with significant others but with an awareness that unless you put yourself first, it is unlikely that other people will healthily do so.

The third basic philosophy that I wish to discuss is called selflessness. If you are selfless, you are basically unconcerned with your own interests and particularly concerned with helping other people achieve their interests. Sometimes when you are selfless, you base your whole existence on putting others first and this gives you meaning in life. You are only basically happy when you are helping other people. However, when you are selfless, mostly you are not so saintly. You would like to put yourself first, but believe that you would be selfish for so doing. Thus, you strive to put others' interests before your own in an attempt to prove how principled you are. Selflessness is very much an attempt to avoid the guilt of putting yourself first, a position that you mistakenly consider to be selfish. Thus, it is here that guilt, namely the belief that you are a selfish, bad person if you put your own interests before others, interferes with putting yourself first in a healthy way.

Let me go over these ideas again because they are so important. When you act selfishly, you consider that there is nothing wrong with putting yourself first under all conditions and you are unconcerned with others. In selflessness, you consider that putting yourself first, before the interests of others, is basically wrong and that you are a selfish, bad person if you do so. In this position, the ethical, principled thing to do is always put others' interests before your own. When you act on the principle of enlightened self-interest, you recognize that putting yourself first on a consistent basis is wrong, but you also hold that there is nothing wrong with putting yourself first to a large, but not exclusive degree. Indeed, you recognize that this is a cornerstone of good mental health. Furthermore, in enlightened self-interest, you are concerned with others and strive to help them achieve their own interests, choosing to put the interests of others first, as long as doing so does not significantly conflict with the pursuit of your own significant interests.

In enlightened self-interest, you are remorseful at others' distress when you put yourself first. In selfishness, you are unconcerned about their distress. In selflessness, you are mortified about their distress, believing that you have caused this by your own selfish actions – which proves that you are a selfish, rotten person.

Guilt, then, plays, the biggest role in leading you to put yourself last. Here, guilt stops you from establishing healthy boundaries between yourself and others, so that you put yourself first much of the time and other people first some of the time. Because there is an unhealthy lack of boundaries between yourself and others, you are easily manipulated by people who want you to put them first on occasions when this significantly conflicts with your own interests.

So if you are a person who would like to pursue your own interests more, but believe that doing so means that you are being selfish, please realize that this is only true if you almost always put yourself first and rarely, if ever, put other people first. Please realize that putting yourself first on a flexible basis is a healthy position and does not mean that you are unconcerned with others. In short, realize that enlightened self-interest is virtually the only way that you will achieve much of what you want, while maintaining good relationships with others.

Can a person's guilt be phoney?

In order to understand the answer to this question, I need to make a distinction between a feeling and an outward expression of that feeling. While it is unlikely that you would have a phoney *feeling* of guilt, it certainly does happen that you may feign guilt in terms of your outward expression of what others may presume to be your guilty feelings. Let me give you an example.

Many years ago one of my students came to a tutorial in a seemingly very distressed state. She said that she had not completed her essay because she had been procrastinating and felt very guilty about her slothful behaviour. Naturally her behaviour elicited a sympathetic response from me, since I was concerned about the extent of her distress. I told her that there was no reason for her to blame herself and if she could understand the basis of her procrastination, she would soon be able to complete her essay. She thanked me profusely and left my office. Ten minutes later I was walking across campus and saw her laughing and joking with other students. I was forcibly struck by her rapid change in mood. I told a colleague about the episode in my office and my observation of the student's sudden change of mood, and he said that he had also experienced something very similar with her.

Several years later I met this ex-student again and we chatted over old times. I mentioned to her about my puzzlement concerning her rapid change of mood, ten minutes after appearing in my office in a very distressed state of mind. She admitted that up to that point in her life, and two years subsequently, she had employed a strategy of appearing to berate herself for some sin or other in order to ward off other people's hostility and to elicit a sympathetic response from them. She admitted that she had not felt at all bad about procrastinating on her essay, but feigned an outward expression of guilt in order to avoid getting into trouble with me. She said that she had learnt about her tendency several years later when she went into therapy and this pattern of feigned guilt had emerged.

It is very difficult for an observer to distinguish between a true expression of guilt and a feigned expression of guilt while it is happening. Indeed, people who feign their outward expression of guilt are frequently very good at dissimulation and are convincing to others. One of the clues that the outward expression of guilt may be being feigned is the rapid change of mood that occurs in the individual after he or she has left the other person with whom he or she feigned guilt.

If you are sure that another person is feigning an outward expression of guilt, then it may be important to bring this to his attention. If I had been aware of my student's tendency to 'put on a guilty face', I would have said something like, 'I'm sorry, but I find it quite difficult to believe that you really do feel as badly about your procrastination as you claim to. I'm not going to blame you, but please be honest with me. Do you really feel as guilty as you appear to feel?' Handling this episode in this way is, of course, a risk because the person's guilt may be genuine. That is why I only suggest this way of dealing with the situation if you are sure that the other person's guilt is feigned. However, if you are correct then this can lead to a more honest relationship between the two of you or to the other person refraining from their manipulative behaviour. Since the major purpose of the feigned expression of guilt is to ward off a hostile, or a blaming response from the other person, it is very important to indicate to the person that whether he is feigning guilt or not, you are not going to blame him for whatever he may have done wrong.

Can guilt be a cover for other feelings?

Yes. In my previous answer I dealt with the issue of phoney guilt. In my response to this question, I want to point out that the guilt that a person experiences is real. However, it may not be the most important emotion being experienced but serves as a legitimate cover for other more central feelings. Let me provide an example.

Marion, a young married woman, came for counselling

61

because she had prolonged feelings of guilt about all the things she had failed to do for her father when he was alive. Her father had died a year previously. During counselling, Marion kept on poring over everything she had failed to do which would have pleased her father in the year before his death. On deeper exploration, it transpired that Marion had always had an ambivalent relationship with her father. On the one hand, she looked up to him; on the other hand, she saw him as an overly restrictive parent. During the counselling process, I helped Marion to identify and work through her feelings of anger towards her father and helped her to accept the fact that he was never the parent that she demanded him to be. Once she had forgiven her father for not giving her the freedom during her late adolescence and early adulthood that she dearly wanted, she could see him in a more human light and began to grieve more healthily for her loss. Having done this, Marion's guilt disappeared, literally overnight.

In this case, Marion's feelings of guilt were masking her feelings of anger. Once she had identified and worked through this anger she was able to grieve her loss without self-blame.

As Tony Gough has shown in his book *Don't Blame Me* (Sheldon Press, 1990), it is important to recognize that guilt can mask other feelings and, in order to determine whether or not this is so, it is important to ask yourself the question 'If I didn't feel guilty, what would I be feeling?' In such instances it is often more acceptable for you to feel guilt than anger, for example. In other instances guilt may be a less threatening emotion than grief. Thus, during counselling, a middle-aged man who had lost a dear friend and felt guilty about all the things he had not done for his friend, discovered that he had not really mourned and cried over his friend's death. Once he had slowly come to terms with his grief, he reported that guilt was a less threatening emotion than grief, since guilt helped him to maintain a sense of control over his emotions. If he were truly to mourn his loss, he feared he would lose control of his feelings. So guilt may not only be a more acceptable emotion to a person than the other feelings it masks, it may also help a person, from his perspective, to gain a sense of control over other feelings.

What is the difference between shame and guilt?

Guilt and shame are frequently confused and here I will describe the similarities and differences between the two emotions. Let me start by comparing existential guilt with existential shame. Earlier in this book I defined existential guilt as an emotion stemming from an enduring belief that one is bad, evil or wicked. Here the content of the enduring self-judgement is that of an immoral self. Existential shame is an enduring belief about oneself as being defective, inadequate and inferior to others. Thus while the similarity between existential guilt and existential shame lies in the fact that in both a negative self-judgement is made, the difference lies in the type of judgement. In guilt, the judgement is about an immoral self whereas in shame it is about a defective, inadequate self.

Let me compare shame and guilt where the negative self-judgements are less enduring and related to specific episodes. You will recall that I distinguish between three types of episodic guilt. The first occurs when you are aware that you have transgressed your moral code or acted in a way that conflicts with your ethical standards. You then believe something like, 'I absolutely should not have transgressed my code and I am a bad person for doing so.' In the second type of episodic guilt, you are aware that you have failed to live up to your moral code. Here your belief is, 'I absolutely should have done what I did not do and I am a bad person for failing to do the right thing.' The third type of episodic guilt occurs when you are aware that you have hurt another person through your actions or what you failed to do. Here your belief is, 'I absolutely should not have hurt the other person and I am an inconsiderate, bad person for doing so.' Thus episodic guilt is related to an actual transgression of a moral code or ethical standard, a failure to live up to an ethical code or moral standard, or the inflicting of some harm on significant others.

In episodic guilt, the role of the other person becomes most salient when you consider that you have inflicted harm on that other person. Here, in this type of episodic guilt, you regard yourself as the source of interpersonal harm. You consider yourself to be both responsible for this harm and to blame for it. The other person, in episodic guilt, is considered to be the injured or hurt party and is held to be dependent, in the sense that her feelings are dependent upon your actions.

In episodic shame, you are aware that you have revealed an inadequacy or an inferiority to other people. However, the role of other people is much more essential to the shame experience than it is in guilt. When you feel ashamed, you infer that one or more people have noticed your revealed inferiority or inadequacy, adopted a scornful or ridiculing attitude towards you and judged you to be inadequate or inferior for revealing the inadequacy or inferiority, a judgement about yourself with which you readily agree.

Let me give a personal example. In my teens I used to have a very bad stammer and was very reluctant to speak in public. I would only speak when absolutely necessary. My wish to conceal my stammer and to hide away from people represents a central aspect in episodic shame. Whenever I did speak in public and inevitably stammered, I considered that I was revealing something inadequate about myself. I would then consider that other people would notice this with a scornful attitude, that is, I believed they judged *me* as inadequate. This only served to confirm my own view about myself, namely that I was inadequate for revealing an inadequacy to other people. In order to overcome my feelings of shame about my stammer and to rid myself of the social anxiety which accompanied it, I had to make various changes in my attitudes towards myself and my interpretations about other people. In fact, I was able to do this over the course of a number of years. I came to learn that even though my stammer may be seen as an inadequacy, I was not an inadequate person for having a stammer. Rather, I was a fallible human being with an unfortunate problem. As I worked on believing this, I became far less likely to mind-read the views of others when they heard me stammering. I recognized that while some people might take a scornful attitude towards me, others would be more sympathetic. I reasoned that even though some people might think I was inadequate for having a stammer, they were wrong about me, and that I could accept myself with my problem in the face of their presumed or actual scorn. As I became more self-accepting about my stammer and thus experienced less shame, I was also less likely to regard myself as being inferior and small, and others as superior and large, which is a typical feature of the experience of shame.

Thus in episodic guilt and episodic shame, the judgements that you make are that you are immoral in guilt and that you are inadequate or unacceptable in shame. In episodic shame, you are concerned that you may reveal an inadequacy or an inferiority in public, whereas in episodic guilt your concern is that you have either broken or failed to live up to a moral code or ethical standard on the one hand and have inflicted interpersonal damage on the other. In episodic shame, the role of the other is much more crucial than in episodic guilt. In shame, you see the other as being strong, the source of contempt and ridicule, and big, whereas you regard yourself as being the object of scorn and ridicule, and small and helpless in the face of the all-powerful, big other. In episodic guilt, the role of the other is most important where you believe that you have inflicted harm on another person. Here, you regard yourself as being responsible and to blame for harming the other, who is seen as being injured, hurt and dependent on your acting morally if he or she is not to experience hurt.

5

Special Kinds of Guilt

In this chapter I examine special kinds of guilt: I explain why people feel guilty about sex, or about surviving the holocaust and other tragedies, and why victims of rape and child sex-abuse feel guilt. Finally, I explain the role that guilt plays in cancer and fear of thunder.

Why do people feel guilty about sex?

While it is probably true that people feel far less guilty about sex these days than they did thirty or forty years ago, some people still feel guilty about sex. Some people still believe that premarital sex is wrong and make themselves guilty about this when they engage in it, while others believe that adulterous sex is wrong and make themselves guilty about having affairs. In both cases, the person experiencing guilt believes that he has either violated an ethical code or harmed another person – be it the person he has had sex with or a third party, namely his spouse (in the case of adultery). Then, believing that he has done the wrong thing, the person makes himself feel guilty about this rather than constructively remorseful. He does this by believing that he absolutely shouldn't have engaged in the sexual activity and that he is a bad person for so doing.

Some people make themselves feel guilty about masturbation because they believe that this activity violates a religious principle. For example, orthodox Jewish men believe that masturbation is wrong and make themselves guilty whenever they engage in it. Their belief that masturbation is wrong stems from olden days when it was considered wrong to spill one's seed which was needed to father sons to be extra pairs of hands to work in the fields. So, when an orthodox Jewish male engages in masturbation he makes himself feel guilty by (a) noting that he has broken a sacred religious principle, and (b) considering himself to be a bad person who absolutely should not have masturbated. There are various solutions open to the orthodox Jewish male to overcome his guilt. First of all, he can refrain from masturbating. (Incidentally, spilling one's seed *involuntarily*, as in one's sleep, is not regarded as a wrongdoing in orthodox Jewish religion.) Second, he can rethink the religious principle and adopt a less orthodox Jewish position which does not regard masturbation as a sin. Finally, he can continue to masturbate and to accept himself for doing so, realizing that he is a fallible human being with natural sexual urges which need expression. Whichever one of these three solutions the orthodox Jewish male adopts, it is far preferable to continuing to masturbate and to feel guilty about it.

What is survivor guilt?

Survivor guilt refers to the feeling of guilt experienced by a person who has survived some negative event of trauma. Survivor guilt encompasses a variety of different reactions which I will exemplify in this response.

Mac was a coal miner who survived an explosion which killed several of his good friends. After he recovered from his injuries, Mac experienced a lot of guilt about the episode. Mac felt guilty about the fact that he survived when other people, who were in his eyes more deserving, did not. Here the idea that the other people who died were more deserving than Mac stemmed from his feelings of guilt and from his tendency to idealize other people. The belief that other people are more deserving than you needs to be closely examined because it may stem from a previous episode about which you feel guilty or from an enduring belief that you are a bad person.

In other instances, you may feel guilty about surviving some trauma because you believe that you are undeserving of your good fortune. This is related to the belief that the world absolutely should not be so unfair as to allow you to survive while other people perished. Another attitude which underpins survivor guilt can be shown in the case of Terry.

Terry was driving on the motorway and his vehicle was hit from behind by a speeding car driven by somebody who had drunk too much alcohol. Terry survived the crash while his three passengers did not. Terry experienced guilt because he believed that he should have died instead of his three friends. Furthermore, he believed that if he had died, then one or more of the others would have survived. This example demonstrates the magical thinking that is involved in survivor guilt: there is no assurance that if Terry had died, one or more of his passengers would have survived.

A belief leading to guilt that is prevalent among survivors of such traumas as the Holocaust or war is: 'Perhaps I could have done something to prevent other people from dying. Since there may have been something that I could have done, I absolutely should have done it and I am a bad person for failing to do what I should have done.' Implicit in this attitude is the idea that you have control over random events and that you should have exercised such control and done something to prevent the death of others. In order to overcome control-related guilt, you need to acknowledge the grim reality that other people with whom we are closely associated may die and that we may survive purely by chance.

A common guilt-related belief that Holocaust survivors often have is that the reason they survived while others died was because they acted in a life-saving but selfish way while others did not and would not have acted so selfishly. In this case, having assumed that his interpretation is true (and that he did act selfishly), the person concerned believes that he absolutely should not have acted selfishly and that he is a bad individual for so doing. Again, this attitude stems largely from the idea: 'Randomness and chance in the world must not exist in such important matters and, since there must be an explanation for why I survived and other people did not, the only possible reason is that I acted selfishly whilst others did not.'

Children of Holocaust survivors also experience guilt. For example, Michael was the only son of two Holocaust survivors and experienced enduring guilt for failing to live up to the expectations of his parents. He had the idea that because his parents had survived such a traumatic ordeal while other people equally deserving did not, then he had to, in some way, validate his parents' survival. The only way he considered that he could do this was by living up to their extraordinary high expectations.

Children of Holocaust survivors often feel guilty about their feelings of resentment towards their parents. On the one hand, they acknowledge that their parents have been through a traumatic experience, and yet on the other they feel angry towards them for their often unreasonable behaviour.

For example, David often experienced a lot of resentment towards his parents who had survived Auschwitz because they had such rigid expectations of him. While he recognized that these rigid expectations may have stemmed from their Holocaust experiences, nevertheless he felt quite angry towards them for being so hard on him. Having realized that he experienced resentment and anger towards his parents, he then made himself guilty because he believed that he abso-lutely must not experience anger towards his parents after all they had suffered, and that he was a bad person for doing so.

In order to overcome survivor guilt, you need to come to terms with the following:

- The fact that you have survived an experience where others died is probably a consequence of chance. Because you survived where others died it does not logically follow that you acted in an immoral way to cheat death.

- If it transpires that you have in fact acted immorally to save yourself, with the result that others may have died, then it is important for you to take responsibility for your behaviour, but to accept yourself for it. Do not condemn yourself.

- The belief that you absolutely should have done something to prevent other people from dying, stems from the idea that the world is an orderly place where events can be prevented by your behaviour. Here again it is important to acknowledge the important role that randomness and chance play in your life. Even if it could be shown that you could have done something to prevent the deaths of others, where is the evidence that you absolutely should have done this and how does it follow that you are a bad, wicked person for failing to do the right thing? As I have shown throughout this book, there is no evidence to uphold the belief that you are a bad person when you fail to uphold your ethical and moral principles. There is only evidence that you are a fallible human being who has done the wrong thing. So accept yourself and learn from your wrongful behaviour.

- Children of Holocaust survivors have a unique burden to bear and yet it is important that they do so without self-defeating guilt. Thus it is important for them to challenge the idea that because their parents suffered a great deal, they absolutely have to make up for this suffering by their own achievements. All they can realistically be expected to do is to strive to fulfil their own potential and if, as a result of this, their parents are disappointed, this is unfortunate but hardly the end of the world.

Surviving trauma of any kind is difficult enough without needless guilt. Indeed, guilt about your survival will interfere with your healthy adaptation to what is, however one looks at it, a difficult situation.

Why do women who have been raped or sexually abused feel guilty?

Let's take the situation of sexual abuse first. When you feel guilty about the fact that you have been sexually abused in your childhood, it is important to recognize that you are looking back upon this experience from the standpoint of an adult. You are, in short, looking at a childhood experience through adult eyes. When you do this, you may well find it difficult to understand your passivity and seeming compliance. Your passivity and apparent compliance was often based on an overwhelming fear that, should you complain, enormous harm would result. If you were sexually abused as a child it is likely that your abuser was someone in whom you placed a great deal of trust. This probably added to your compliance. It is important to remember these things when you look back at those experiences.

When you feel guilty about your failure to prevent such abuse, you first believe that you were wrong not to prevent the abuse, and second, that you absolutely should not have done the wrong thing and that you are bad for failing to do what you absolutely should have done. When you hold such beliefs it is difficult if not impossible to take a compassionate, understanding view of your passivity.

Some theorists in the field argue that guilt related to sexual abuse is a result of dealing with your powerlessness. Here, you believe, 'I absolutely should have been more powerful in order to prevent the abuse.' Similar attitudes are held by people who feel guilty as a result of being raped. If this applies to you it is likely that you believe that you absolutely should have been able to do something to prevent the rape and that you are bad for failing to take such preventative action. In addition, you may well find it difficult to comprehend the randomness of such an attack. In reality you were literally in the wrong place at the wrong time. But you may catch yourself saying something like 'If only I had not walked down that dark alleyway when I did', or 'If only I had worn different clothing then this wouldn't have happened'. These ideas stem from the view a) that negative events can be prevented and b) that you absolutely should act in such a way as to prevent them. If you have been raped, it is very important for you to acknowledge that, even if you acted in a way which, retrospectively, you construe to be risky, this does not mean that you are responsible for a sexual attack or rape. Let me be quite clear on this. No matter where a woman walks, if she is raped, it is the sole responsibility of the rapist.

Sarah was raped as she was going into her flat. She was attacked from behind, pushed into her flat, forced to engage in indecent sexual acts, and then raped. Sarah believed quite categorically that there must have been something that she could have done to prevent this attack. This guilt-creating philosophy led her to go over and over the minutes before the attack in her mind in search of something not only that she *could have done*, but that she *absolutely should have done*, to prevent the attack. In counselling, I helped Sarah to appreciate that her obsessive search for something that she could have done to prevent the rape was based on the idea that she absolutely should be able to have perfect control over her environment and on the related belief that it is horrible if traumatic incidents occur as a consequence of chance. I helped her to realize that while it would have been nice if she could have done something to prevent it, she was a fallible human being and that there's no reason to believe that she absolutely should have done something to prevent it. She learned that her failure to prevent this rape did not mean that she is impotent and unable to cope with other life events – a frequent idea which accompanies control-related guilt. I also helped Sarah to accept the grim fact that as her attacker was far more physically powerful than her, there would have been little she could do about it, even if she had not been in a state of shock. This acknowledgement led her to join a judo club to help her empower herself as a single woman living alone.

Laura was sexually abused by an uncle of whom she was very fond. She felt guilty because she remembered sitting on his lap and hugging him and not telling anybody of the abuse after it had occurred. Laura believed that she absolutely should not have done what she did, that she absolutely should have screamed to stop the abuse and that she absolutely should have told somebody afterwards. Laura's case is a good example of an adult looking back on a childhood experience with adult eyes. When I encouraged her to adopt the frame of mind of the young child Laura who experienced this abuse, she realized that she did not appreciate that she was doing the wrong thing and, as a result of trusting her uncle, she could not have believed that he would betray her trust. Even though she remembered having a dim awareness at the time that there was something wrong happening, she was scared when her uncle swore her to secrecy. As a result, Laura realized that she could have only acted as she did and there was no reason why she absolutely should have acted any differently, even though it would have been better if she had. She began to appreciate fully the fact that she acted the way she did because she was a child at the time and she did so originally because she trusted her uncle and latterly because she was scared of what would happen, should she disclose their 'secret'.

Finally, let me consider the case of Sandra, who was raped on a building site, having been attacked and abducted by two men. Sandra's guilt centred around the fact that she had an orgasm during the assault. In her mind the fact that she experienced an orgasm meant that she had done something to bring about the situation. The experience of female orgasm during rape is not an uncommon experience. It is not only something which is very confusing for the victim but it often leads to a lot of emotional distress. The way I explain this phenomenon to women is that our bodies often respond in ways which are unrelated to the wishes of our conscious minds. Thus, women who dearly want to experience an orgasm with men whom they love and adore very often fail to experience an orgasm in such situations, whereas women who really do not want to experience an orgasm in other situations, do so. Often, our bodies respond according to how we are being stimulated, not according to our conscious desires. So under certain circumstances, orgasm is not a reflection of how you feel emotionally towards another person, but rather a result of the way your body is being stimulated. Discussing such points with Sandra helped her to appreciate that her orgasmic response was not a reflection of her feelings towards her attacker and was certainly not a reflection of any unconscious desire to be attacked in this way. Rather, it was a matter of her body reacting to stimulation of a certain kind, a reflection of the fact that she does not have perfect control over her bodily responses.

Is guilt involved in whether or not a person fights an illness such as cancer?

The answer to this question is that guilt can be a factor in whether or not a person fights an illness such as cancer or other life-threatening disease, although it is fairly rare. I have consulted several of my colleagues who work as counsellors with those who have a life-threatening illness, and their experience concurs with mine in that guilt sometimes, but infrequently, plays a part in the recovery process. Parents of children with a handicap often feel guilty in that they believe that they must have done something wrong to deserve having a handicapped child. A similar situation sometimes occurs when people have a serious illness such as cancer.

Patricia was diagnosed as having cancer of the breast and, after she recovered from the shock, she plunged into a black state of guilty despair. She told her counsellor that she believed that she contracted cancer as a result of an affair of several years earlier, which she had managed to keep secret, but about which she felt very guilty. Understanding the psychological dynamics of guilt can help to explain this phenomenon. As stated throughout this book, guilt is a feeling that stems from the idea that you absolutely must not violate your moral code and that you are a bad person for so doing. In addition, since you are a bad person, you deserve to be punished for your 'sin'. Once Patricia was helped to get over this guilt-creating philosophy and was helped to accept herself for breaking her moral code, this freed her to understand why she had had the affair. She learned that she was dissatisfied with her relationship with her husband who worked very long hours and she considered that she was being neglected. This insight deepened her self-acceptance with the result that she got over the idea that her breast cancer was a form of punishment for her adultery. As her guilt lessened, she was more determined to live more honestly and, three years later, she divorced her husband and on medical follow-up was given a clean bill of health from her consultant.

I've heard that guilt is involved in the fear of thunder. Is this true?

Yes, it can be true, but like the role that guilt plays in whether or not a person fights a life-threatening illness, it is fairly rare. During the twenty years that I have practised as a counsellor, I can recall only two cases where fear of thunder was based on guilt. I will describe one of these cases to show how guilt may be involved in thunder phobia.

Teresa was a 44-year-old Catholic woman who came to me because her life had become increasingly incapacitated by a fear of thunderstorms. She would anxiously scan weather reports and if there was even the slightest hint of a thunderstorm on the horizon, she would refuse to go out and insist that her husband and children stay with her in the house. At the first sign of a storm she would put on all the lights and switch on the television, her hi-fi equipment, and all the transistor radios in the house in order to block out the thunder. In treating the fear of thunder, I usually expect to find some experience where the person, as a child, was extremely frightened by a thunderstorm. However, in Teresa's case, I could not find such a conditioning experience. After a fairly lengthy assessment, it emerged that Teresa felt very guilty about stealing some money from a coworker's purse five years previously. It was at this date that her fear of thunder started. Teresa believed that she was a bad person for stealing the money in that she had violated a moral code and believed that, under no circumstances, should she have acted in the way that she did. It further transpired that around that time, Teresa was depressed because her husband had lost his job and she was very worried about the family's financial situation. I first helped her to accept herself for her moral code violation and helped her to understand the context in which she acted in the way she did. I then helped her to understand that her belief that she was a bad person further led her to believe that she deserved the wrath of God for her sin. In her mind, thunder was God's way of communicating to her that he was aware of her sin and condemned her for it. Having helped her to accept herself for her sin, I also encouraged her to appreciate that she really believed in a loving compassionate God who would understand her actions and would want her to make amends. Teresa decided to admit her sin to the co-worker concerned, to return the money with interest, and to ask for forgiveness and understanding in an adult-to-adult way. To her great surprise, her co-worker was overwhelmed by her courage, forgave her for her sin and disclosed how she herself had been tempted to steal money from another person when her family was short of money. Having accepted herself for stealing her co-worker's money, and having been forgiven by her, Teresa completely lost her fear of thunder, since there was no further reason to believe that God was angry with her.

Thus, if you are afraid of thunder and cannot easily find a good reason to explain this fear, it is worth while asking yourself whether you have done something in your life that you feel guilty about and for which you believe God will punish you. It may well be that you associate thunder with the wrath of God.

6

Partial Solutions
to Guilt

In the following chapter, I show the way in which people try to cope with guilt and why these are only partial solutions to the problem. Specifically, I discuss the role of confession, being forgiven by others, and reassurance.

Is confession healthy?

In my view, confession is a partial solution to the problem of guilt, along with other partial solutions such as repenting your sins, praying for forgiveness and making amends for your sins. The reason why I consider such activities to be only partial solutions to overcoming guilt is that none of these activities helps you to identify, challenge and change your guilt-creating philosophy which, in my view, is at the core of the guilt experience. When you confess your sins to a priest, he listens silently to what you have to say and then absolves you of your sin. In addition, you may be asked to show your repentance in some way. However, as I have emphasized in this book, guilt comes from the idea that you absolutely should not have acted in the way that you did, and that you are a bad person for so doing. When you confess your sins and are given absolution, you may well change your belief to 'I am not a bad person *because* I have confessed my sins and have received absolution'. Thus your self-acceptance is conditional upon the act of confession and receiving absolution and you still retain the philosophy that if you committed a sin, did not confess and did not receive absolution, then you would still be a bad person.

The same also applies to the act of praying for forgiveness.

When you pray to God for forgiveness, you are again acknowledging your sins in the eyes of the Lord and you make the
assumption that God will forgive you for your sins. So again, your
new attitude is that 'I am not a bad person because God has
forgiven me'. In doing so, you retain the underlying attitude that
you would be a bad person if you did not pray for forgiveness
and, indeed, did not receive it from God.

When you carry out an act of reparation which involves you
making amends for your sin, you again only partially change your
guilt-creating philosophy. Thus, you still believe that you are a
bad person for doing what you absolutely should not have done
and will continue to be a bad person, unless you make amends for
your sin. Indeed, if you carry out an act of reparation, without
first changing your guilt-creating philosophy, the danger is that
you may make amends in a way which is disproportionate to your
sin. If you have harmed another person, you may beg the other
person for forgiveness, rather than asking for forgiveness in an
adult-to-adult fashion.

If you wish to confess your sins, carry out an act of repentance
and reparation, or pray for forgiveness, I recommend that you
first identify, challenge and change your guilt-creating idea: 'I
absolutely should not have acted in the way that I did and I am a
bad person for so doing.' After you have accepted or forgiven
yourself for your sin, then by all means confess your sin to a
priest, repent the sin, pray for forgiveness or make amends to
another person. Doing it in this order ensures that your
confession etc. is based on healthy self-acceptance, not on a
desperate attempt to rid yourself of unhealthy self-blame.

Does being forgiven by another person help people stop feeling guilty?

I have partially answered this question in relation to praying to
God for forgiveness. I showed in that answer that ridding
yourself of guilt by assuming that God has forgiven you does not

help you to accept yourself for your sin, in the event that you think that God will not forgive you.

Similarly, when you have wronged another person, it may be healing to ask that person to forgive you. If the person does forgive you, then your self-acceptance is conditional upon being forgiven. In this case, you still retain the idea that you are a bad person unless you are forgiven. A more comprehensive solution to the problem of guilt is, as I have shown above, to forgive yourself for your sins, whether or not you are forgiven by others. This unconditional self-acceptance is particularly important when the person you have wronged refuses to forgive you. If you adopt a philosophy of conditional self-acceptance, you are still left with underlying feelings of guilt because you still believe that you are a bad person unless you are forgiven by the other person. However, when you fully and unconditionally accept yourself for your sin, you can, in short, forgive yourself for the wrong that you have done the other person, even if he or she does not.

In conclusion, it is healthier for you to believe that you can forgive yourself, whether or not you are forgiven by another, than it is for you to believe that you can forgive yourself only if you are forgiven by the other person.

Why do I only feel better temporarily when someone shows me that I haven't done anything wrong?

When you tell others what you feel guilty about, two of the most common responses you are likely to receive from them are attempts to show you (1) that what you consider to be wrong was not, in fact, wrong or (2) that there were justifiable reasons why you acted in the way you did. Both of these responses are well-intentioned and as you imply in the question, they do help you to feel better in the short run. However, as you correctly note, this is frequently only a temporary solution to the problem of guilt. The reason why it is temporary is that such responses are not based on your frame of reference but on the other person's. Thus, from the point of view of the other person you may not have done the wrong thing, or there may be good reasons why you did what you did. The seductive aspect of this is that the other person's argument may be persuasive *at the time*. I have emphasized the phrase 'at the time' because later, when you are on your own again and you do not have the other person around to reassure you, you either forget about his or her arguments, or you counteract them in your mind.

Let me illustrate this by discussing the case of Lesley. Lesley had successfully dieted and maintained her weight loss over a lengthy period. However, one day she had a disagreement with a colleague at work, became very upset, and immediately went on an extended binge. After she had managed to stop the binge, she became tremendously guilty for what she considered to be her gluttonous behaviour. Lesley and her friends had always been able to confide in one another about their personal problems and, on this occasion, Lesley spent a long time talking to her friends about her guilt. Some of her friends tried to help Lesley by showing her that what she had done wasn't really wrong and by reminding her how successful she had been by adhering to the diet for so long. These friends encouraged her to regard the binge as only a slight lapse rather than an example of gluttonous behaviour. Lesley found herself initially comforted by these arguments but afterwards, when she thought back over the event, she returned to her view that she acted gluttonously and again made herself feel guilty about her behaviour.

Then, Lesley spoke to other friends who used a different argument with her. They encouraged her to look at her behaviour in context. Their argument was that it was quite understandable for Lesley to go on a binge because she was in a very distressed, emotional state. We all tend to overeat when we are upset, they reminded her. Once again Lesley felt reassured, but again this reassurance did not last. She reflected on the episode and considered that the emotional upset that she experienced was an overreaction to the situation with the co-worker and, in any case, that was no real excuse for her overeating. She then returned to making herself feel guilty for her so-called gluttonous behaviour.

I hope you can see, then, that when other people try to show you that you haven't done something wrong, or explain to you that there is a very good reason for your wrongdoing, this will temporarily relieve your guilt and reassure you. However, this is not a lasting solution to the problem of guilt. The more permanent solution to overcoming guilt involves you first assuming, temporarily, that what you did was wrong and then identifying, challenging and changing the guilt-creating beliefs which you bring to this event. I will discuss this more fully in the next chapter when I outline a step-by-step guide to overcoming guilt.

7

Getting over Guilt

In this final chapter, I discuss more productive ways of dealing with guilt and offer a step-by-step guide to successfully overcoming guilt.

If I feel guilty when I do not live up to my moral or ethical standards, should I lower my standards, change my behaviour or change my attitude?

My advice on this point is, first, to change your attitude about your failure to live up to your moral or ethical standards before considering lowering these standards and before you try to change your future behaviour. If you try to lower your standards or change your behaviour *before* you change your guilt-creating attitude, then your decision-making will still be influenced by guilt. For example, if you do not change your guilt-creating attitude first, while you are considering how far to lower your standards, or when you are thinking about how you might change your future behaviour, you will be still influenced by the idea that you absolutely must live up to your standards and that you are a bad person for failing to do so. Thus, if you do not change your guilt-creating philosophy first, even though you may lower your standards, you will make yourself guilty whenever you fail to live up to even these lowered standards.

However, if you first change your guilt-creating philosophy and challenge the idea that you absolutely must live up to your standards and that you are a bad person if you do not, you will then be in a much better frame of mind to make healthy decisions about how far to lower your standards and how you can improve your future behaviour. Furthermore, if you do decide to lower your standards, having first changed your guilt-creating philosophy, you will be far less likely to make yourself guilty if you fail to live up to these lowered standards.

Also, if you are considering changing your behaviour when you are still underlyingly guilty, you will be motivated to avoid thinking about your past wrongdoings because you would experience guilt if you were to do so.

As I have already discussed, feeling guilty prevents you from looking objectively at your past wrongful behaviour and from understanding the factors that led you to act in the way you did. In contrast, feeling constructively remorseful about your past wrongful behaviour – a feeling which is based on the idea that you are a fallible human being when you act wrongfully and that there is no law of the universe to say that you absolutely must not do the wrong thing – motivates you to understand why you acted in the way you did, and what are some of the factors that influenced you in your decision to act wrongfully. Then you can usefully learn from this experience and plan to change your future behaviour accordingly. In addition, when you feel constructive remorse rather than unconstructive guilt, if you then fail to act ethically, you would still accept yourself for this failure and learn constructive lessons from it. However, when you bring your guilt-creating philosophy to your failure to act in the ethical way you had planned, you then make yourself feel guilty about this because you believe: 'Now I have resolved to act more ethically, I absolutely must do so and I am a bad person if I fail to meet my new ethical goals.'

To conclude, first challenge your guilt-creating ideas and replace these with a less demanding, more self-accepting philosophy about your wrongful behaviour. Then learn from your experience, either by planning to act ethically in future or by lowering your standards, if this is appropriate. Lowering your standards is particularly useful when these standards are in-human and perfectionist in nature. For example, if you have a standard never to harm another human being, this is unrealistic since, as long as you are involved with other people, there is no guarantee that other people will not be upset about something that you have done or failed to do.

How important is it to re-evaluate our values as a way of getting over guilt?

I would say that re-evaluating your values forms a part of getting over guilt, but it is by no means the whole story. In fact, my answer to this question is similar to the one I provided to the previous question. First, assume that your moral value is relevant and, when you have acted in a way that conflicts with this value, acknowledge that you have done something wrong. Then, work to identify, challenge and change your guilt-creating attitudes. Having then accepted yourself for your presumed wrongdoing, you are in a far better position to question how relevant your moral value still is. If you try to question the relevance of your moral value when you are experiencing guilt, you will often bias your answer in the direction of believing that what is really an outmoded moral value is still relevant to you.

Why is questioning your moral values an important thing to do? The answer to this lies in your human tendency to accept unquestioningly the values of your parents and other authorities when you are young. Psychologists call these introjected values. This term reflects the idea that you 'swallow whole' the moral teachings of your parents, teachers and other authorities, without 'chewing' them over and considering whether or not they are relevant to you. The tendency to introject values unthinkingly is probably a natural tendency during childhood. However, continuing to believe in introjected moral values, without rethinking them, is, in my opinion, not a sign of good mental health. Thinking for yourself *is* mentally healthy and consequently, asking yourself why an activity is bad is a useful antidote to uncritically accepting the views of significant others.

Let me discuss the case of Peter to illustrate this point. Peter came to see me because he was troubled by some of his sexual thoughts towards women. He had split up from his wife two years previously and was becoming increasingly sexually frustrated. When he first consulted me, Peter had no current woman friend in his life. He increasingly believed that if he did not get sexual release soon, he would lose control of himself and perhaps carry out a sexual attack on a female stranger. As part of my assessment of this problem, I asked Peter how frequently he masturbated. He gave me a look of horror and said, 'I don't engage in that disgusting practice. It's wrong.' 'Oh,' I asked, 'what's wrong about it?' Peter thought long and hard and could not answer my question. In his struggle to come up with an acceptable reply, Peter said that he had been taught by his scout leader, his priest and his father that masturbation was wrong and had accepted their opinion on the matter. Having led a fairly active sex life with his wife, he had no need to gain sexual release in any way other than through intercourse.

Peter's case is a good example of what Tony Gough in his book *Don't Blame Me* has shown to be an important factor in the maintenance of introjected values – that we come to believe something is wrong because our parents and other significant authorities would not approve of the activity. Just because your parents and others do not approve of a particular activity, does not mean that it is morally wrong. In Peter's case, I asked him whether he believed that God would be offended if he masturbated. Peter thought for a while and said, 'No, I don't believe that God would.' I then asked Peter who would be harmed if he masturbated. Again, Peter thought for a moment and replied, 'Nobody'.

I then explained to Peter the origin of the taboo against masturbation, which I discussed earlier in the book (see pp. 66–7). I suggested to him that he write down the reasons why *he* believed masturbation was wrong. The next week, Peter arrived for our session with a blank sheet of paper and was far less tense than in our first session. Having reflected on the question 'is masturbation wrong?', Peter realized that he had uncritically accepted this value from his elders who would not approve of this activity. He thus reformulated his moral value and was able to experience release from his sexual tension with an accompanying significant decrease in his sexual preoccupations with attacking women.

If you believe that some of your values are outmoded, it is worth while asking yourself similar questions to those I asked Peter: 'Why is this activity wrong?' 'Who would be harmed if I carried out the activity?' – and, most significantly, 'Would my parents and other significant authorities approve of this activity?' If you come to see that an activity is based on an outmoded moral value which you are sustaining in order to gain the approval of significant others in your life and for no other reason, it may be helpful to challenge the idea that you must not be disapproved of by these other people. Realize that part of being mentally healthy is living life according to your own deeply held values, rather than on values which are deeply held by other people.

In conclusion, let me remind you of the sequence I have outlined in this answer. First, assume that your moral value is still current and that you have in fact violated your moral code. Second, identify, challenge and change your guilt-creating attitudes, and allow yourself to feel remorse about your code violation. Third, free from guilt, question whether your moral value is personally meaningful or one that you have introjected from people who would disapprove of the behaviour prohibited by the moral value.

If a good friend of mine acted in the same way as me, I wouldn't condemn her. So, why do I condemn myself and feel guilty for the very same thing?

I have often found that people are more compassionate and understanding when their friends do the wrong thing than they are towards themselves, when they act in the self-same way. Why is this? When your friend commits a sin, and you do not condemn her for her behaviour, you have a different attitude towards her than you have towards yourself when you do the same thing. Thus, you believe that while it may have been desirable for your friend not to have acted badly, she is not a bad person for so doing. However, when you act in exactly the same way you believe that there is a law of the universe that states that you absolutely should not have done what you did and that you are a bad person as a result. In short, you have a non-demanding attitude towards your friend and accept her as a fallible human being who can do and has done the wrong thing. However, you have a demanding attitude towards yourself and you refuse to acknowledge that you are a fallible human being who has acted wrongfully.

If you inspect closely this different set of beliefs, you will discover an interesting point. What you are saying about your friend is that she is a fallible human being who is allowed to make mistakes, but that you should be super-human and not make the same mistakes. In a sense, you are treating yourself as if you are god-like. Failing to achieve your god-like status, you then consider that you are a devil – literally a bad person who absolutely should not have acted in the human manner that you did. By doing this you completely overlook the fact that 'to sin is human, to forgive yourself, divine'.

Thus, when you are compassionate towards your friend, you are treating her as a fallible human being who has done the wrong thing. When you fail to show compassion towards yourself, you are demanding that you should be above human fallibility and if you are not above fallibility, i.e. god-like, you are below fallibility, i.e. wicked and bad. Thus, to show yourself the same level of compassion as you do your friend, you need to challenge the idea that you must be godlike and you need to accept yourself as a fallible human being, equal in humanity with all other humans.

Let me discuss the case of Victoria to illustrate these points. At the age of 17, Victoria became pregnant and decided, after much thought, to have an abortion. Although she regarded

88

abortion as wrong, she realized that as a young, single person, she was ill-equipped to become a mother. However, as soon as she had had the abortion she became extremely guilty. She not only made herself guilty about breaking her moral code (i.e. having an abortion), she also made herself guilty about acting in a very selfish way, by choosing to put her rights ahead of the rights of her unborn child. Victoria was referred to me for counselling after she had been given several different anti-depressant drugs and had seen her church minister. However, neither the medication nor her priest could help her to relieve her immense guilt. After several fruitless discussions, I managed to help Victoria relinquish her self-defeating guilt in the following way.

WINDY: So, Victoria, you are convinced that you are a bad person on two counts. First, for having the abortion, and second, for putting your rights ahead of your unborn child. Have I understood you correctly?

VICTORIA: That sums up exactly how I do feel.

WINDY: Who is your best friend?

VICTORIA: Her name is Samantha and I'm very close to her.

WINDY: Let me put a point to you. Let's suppose that Samantha became pregnant and decided to have an abortion. No doubt, as soon as you learnt of this you would go up to her and tell her that she was a wicked person for committing a mortal sin.

VICTORIA: What do you mean? I wouldn't say that to her. She's my best friend.

WINDY: You wouldn't say that to her face, but would you think that she was a wicked person for having the abortion?

VICTORIA: No. As I said before, she's my friend.

WINDY: Well, why wouldn't you think that she was a wicked person? After all, she would have had an abortion.

VICTORIA: Well, Samantha wouldn't do anything to harm a

fly. She's very kind towards other people, so of course she's not a bad person.

WINDY: Even though she committed what you consider to be a heinous act?

VICTORIA: No. Not even then. I can say, without a shadow of doubt, that I wouldn't consider Samantha to be a wicked person.

WINDY: So let me get this straight. You have an abortion and act in a way that you regard as selfish, and you are wicked. Samantha does exactly the same thing and she's not wicked. How do you explain this discrepancy?

VICTORIA: Wait a minute, you're confusing me. I don't understand what you mean.

WINDY; Well you seem to have a double standard here. On the one hand, you're saying that even if Samantha did exactly the same thing as you, i.e. have an abortion and act in a way that you consider selfish, you wouldn't condemn her because she has other good traits. The way I'd put it, you would regard her as a fallible human being, who had done the wrong thing. You would still see what she did as wrong, but she would not be a bad person. Is that right?

VICTORIA: Yes. I think I'm beginning to see what you mean.

WINDY: You commit exactly the same act, and act in exactly the same 'selfish' way, and you are a bad person. Do you see that you are really saying that you should be above Samantha in the way you act? She's allowed to be human and you're not.

VICTORIA: I've never looked at it like that before. I guess that's exactly what I'm doing.

WINDY: So, if I could only get you to treat yourself in the same human way that you would treat Samantha, then you would be able to move forward. Now, don't get me wrong. I am not suggesting that you minimize the 'sin' that you have committed. Nor, for a moment, am I trying to convince you that you haven't acted selfishly. We'll talk about that later.

But if you could accept yourself as a human being who has done the wrong thing, you will feel what I call constructively remorseful, and not self-defeatingly guilty. This will help you to understand why you had the abortion in the first place, since as long as you insist on condemning yourself as a bad, wicked person, how can you possibly begin to understand, in a compassionate way, why you decided to do what you did?

VICTORIA: So what you are saying is that I should learn to treat myself in the same human way as I would treat Samantha. You're not suggesting that abortion is right or that I didn't act in a selfish way?

WINDY: No, I'm assuming, for the time being, that you have broken your moral code and have acted selfishly. What I am suggesting is that you forgive yourself for that in the same way as you would forgive Samantha.

VICTORIA: Well, that certainly makes sense and I'm certainly prepared to give it a try.

Using these arguments with herself, Victoria helped herself to overcome her guilt and began to adopt a self-accepting philosophy towards her 'sin'. She still regarded her abortion as a sin, but because she wasn't condemning herself as she did previously, she was able to take a more compassionate attitude towards her behaviour and understand that she made her decision at a time when she was scared, frightened and desperate, and when she was all alone.

Victoria's story demonstrates something that I have found time and time again. That when you condemn yourself for breaking your moral code, you are ensuring that guilt does not allow you to realize that there may be mitigating circumstances which help explain why you acted in the way you did. However, when you begin to accept yourself for your 'sin', you are then in a better emotional and objective frame of mind to take into account any mitigating circumstances that existed which may have influenced your behaviour.

How can I tell how bad my 'sin' is?

Your question raises the issue of how you can put things into perspective. There are various techniques that you can use to do this and I do recommend that you use some of them. However, in keeping with the argument that I have used throughout this book, I recommend that you do this *after* you have overcome your feelings of guilt by identifying, challenging and changing your guilt-creating ideas. I recommend this order because when you experience guilt, this feeling will bias your attempts to put matters into perspective and will frequently stop you from being logical and objective – two qualities you need if you are to benefit fully from perspective-taking techniques.

Let me assume, then, that you have identified the events about which you are making yourself feel guilty. You have also identified your guilt-creating ideas, have challenged them and have begun to feel remorseful about your 'sin' rather than guilty. What can you then do to take a more objective look at your behaviour and judge how bad it actually was?

The first method I suggest that you use is called the 'continuum of badness' technique. Draw a vertical line on a piece of paper and write '100% bad', at the top of the line and '0% bad' at the bottom. Now, further divide the line by putting checkmarks against '25% bad', '50% bad' and '75% bad' (see figure 1).

Figure 1: The continuum of badness

Now, concentrate on your act and write down how bad you think it was by putting a cross on the line. Then think of the most heinous crime that you can imagine *anyone* committing. Really use your imagination and write it, the ultimate sin, at the top of the line, next to '100% bad'. Now think of a number of other sins ranging from the serious to the not so serious, and write them down on the line next to the appropriate percentage mark. Having done this, go back to your original act and, being as objective as you can, compare it with the ultimate sin and with the other sins that you have checked, and decide again how bad it is when judged against these other sins. In all probability, your second rating will be less severe than your original rating.

The purpose of this technique is not to absolve you of responsibility for what you have done but to help you to put it into a broad moral context.

The second technique that you can use is the 'one day to live' technique which Vernon Coleman describes in his book *How to Stop Feeling Guilty* (Sheldon Press, 1982). Here you focus on your behaviour and imagine how bad it is when viewed from the perspective of having one day left to live. In all probability, under these circumstances, you would not consider your behaviour to be nearly as bad as you do now.

A similar technique is called time projection. Here, you imagine that you have access to a time machine in which you can travel into the future. First ask yourself how bad you consider your behaviour to be now. Then, get into your time machine and imagine that it is now five years into the future. From that perspective, how badly do you think you have behaved? Ask yourself the same question ten years from now, twenty years from now, until you see that your judgements are affected by time. What you consider to be a heinous crime now, you will probably judge more leniently and with greater compassion later.

Again, use this technique after you have first identified,

challenged and changed your guilt-creating ideas. Doing this will enable you to be sufficiently objective to get the most out of these techniques, just described.

The techniques that I have discussed so far are most useful when it is clear that you have exaggerated the badness of your behaviour. They are not so helpful in situations when it is clear, no matter how you view it, that you have committed a serious sin. How can you possibly forgive yourself when you have committed a dreadful sin? The answer is by applying exactly the same techniques that I have discussed in this book. First, acknowledge that you have acted immorally. Realize that human beings are capable of a great number of different atrocities and there is no point minimizing this fact. However, if you have committed such an atrocity it is crucial that you learn from your experience and not commit similar atrocities in the future. In order to do this, it is essential that you forgive yourself for your atrocious behaviour.

Let's take an example. Stanley came for counselling after being confronted by his adult stepdaughter. She accused him of sexually abusing her when she was in her early teens. Stanley had acknowledged that he had committed the abuse and felt so badly about himself that he took an overdose of tablets, slashed his wrists and locked himself in the bathroom. Fortunately for Stanley, the lock on the bathroom door was faulty and his wife was able to break the lock and save his life. During counselling, I never once sought to minimize Stanley's behaviour, which I agreed was indeed extremely bad. However, I was able to show Stanley that his behaviour was due to a combination of poor impulse control and emotional disturbance, and that if everybody in life who suffered from similar problems were to be condemned to death, the world's population would be much smaller than it is today. I reminded Stanley that he would have to live with his behaviour for the rest of his life, yet he could do so with proper and constructive remorse without self-defeating and, in his case, life-threatening guilt.

I wish to stress that this approach to helping people who have abused others or who have committed other atrocities is one that I consider to be humane. It involves encouraging the person (a) to take full responsibility for what he has done; (b) to recognize that what he did was extremely bad; (c) to see his actions as evidence of significant emotional disturbance and (d) to accept himself as a human being who is disturbed rather than as a wicked person who deserves to be severely punished, and, in Stanley's case, condemned to death. When people accept themselves for their sins, even very serious ones, they can then reflect on their behaviour and understand why they acted as they did. This helps them to learn from the experience and minimize the chances that they will act in an abusive or atrocious manner in the future.

I am quite clear that if I did not help Stanley to accept himself (but not his behaviour), either he would have committed suicide or he would have continued to act in a wicked, evil manner consistent with the way he viewed himself.

Can you suggest a step-by-step guide to overcome guilt?

I will first answer this question by outlining a step-by-step guide to help you to overcome episodic guilt.

STEP 1: *Identify your feeling of guilt and don't confuse it with another feeling* (such as shame).

STEP 2: *Identify any secondary emotional problem that you have about your feeling of guilt* (e.g. anger at yourself for feeling guilty). If you find a secondary problem, deal with it first. Show yourself that there's no law of the universe that says that you must not feel guilty even though it is self-defeating. Remind yourself that while it is desirable for you not to feel guilty, it does not follow that therefore you must not feel guilty. If you're feeling guilty, that's reality and it is like that because you have a guilt-creating philosophy. Recognize that even though feeling guilty may be self-defeating, you are not a stupid person for acting in such a self-defeating manner. If you were a stupid person, everything that you could possibly do would be stupid. Rather, you are a fallible human being who is doing a self-defeating thing. Overcoming your secondary emotional problem about feeling guilty is important in that doing so will help you to focus your attention on overcoming your primary problem, namely your guilt.

STEP 3: *Identify what it is that you feel most guilty about*. Be as clear and as specific as you can when thinking about what you feel most guilty about. Remind yourself that guilt is related to:

- an action which violates your moral code;
- something you have not done which constitutes a failure to live up to your moral code or ethical principle;
- an action which has 'hurt' another person's feelings or caused them to be harmed in some way.

At this stage, assume that it is true that you have acted wrongfully.

STEP 4: *Identify your guilt-creating attitudes*. In particular, identify the demand that you are making of yourself. Ask yourself, am I demanding that I must not violate my moral code? Am I demanding that I must live up to my moral code or ethical principle, or am I demanding that I must not cause harm to other people?

Second, identify your guilt-creating attitudes towards yourself. Ask yourself, am I evaluating myself as a bad or wicked person for acting in the way that I absolutely should not? Do I consider that I deserve to be punished for my sins?

STEP 5: *Appreciate the central role that attitudes play in guilt*. Recognize that it is these unconstructive guilt-creating attitudes that are at the core of the guilt experience and that you need to challenge and change them in order to feel constructively remorseful, rather than self-defeatingly guilty.

STEP 6: *Challenge your guilt-creating attitudes*. It is important to challenge each of the guilt-creating attitudes that you have identified by asking three questions: Does this attitude lead to healthy emotional results? Is it logical? Is it consistent with reality?

Let's take your belief 'I absolutely must not break my moral code' and apply each of the three questions to it.

- *Does this attitude lead to good results?* No. As long as you demand that you must not violate your moral code you will feel guilty and this belief will interfere with your learning why you broke your moral code in the first place.

- *It is logical?* No. While it is perfectly healthy for you to believe that it would have been preferable for you not to violate your moral code, it does not logically follow that you absolutely must not. Absolute musts hardly every follow logically from undemanding preferences. Thus, if you believe that it would be nice for a thousand pounds to drop into your lap right now, it is quite clearly illogical to demand that it therefore absolutely has to. In the same way, just because you would healthily prefer not to violate your moral code, it is illogical for you to conclude that you must not violate it.

- *Is your demand consistent with reality?* No. If there was a law of the universe that declared that you absolutely must not violate your moral code, then it would be impossible for you to do so. This is because you would have to follow such a universal law. However, since we know that you did violate your moral code, we can say that your demand that you must not do so is inconsistent with reality.

In conclusion, in answer to your three questions, you can see that your demand that you must not break your moral code is unhelpful, illogical and inconsistent with reality. However, the healthy alternative to this belief, namely, 'I would much prefer not to break my moral code but unfortunately there is no law of the universe that says that I must not', is more helpful in that it would lead to constructive remorse rather than self-defeating guilt, it is logical and it is consistent with reality.

Now, let's take your belief 'I am a bad person for violating my moral code', and apply the same three questions.

- *Is this belief helpful?* Here the answer is clearly no. As long as you think of yourself as a bad person, (a) you will feel guilty about your moral code violation, (b) your guilt will again interfere with your learning why you violated your code in the first place, and (c) you increase the likelihood that you will act in a way that is consistent with this self-definition. In other words, you increase, rather than reduce the chances of acting badly in the future.

- *Is it logical?* Here you are saying that since you have done a bad thing, this makes you a bad person. This is clearly illogical because it is an over-generalization. You begin with something which may well be true, namely that you have done something wrong, and you conclude wrongly that this action makes the whole of you bad.

- *Is this belief consistent with reality?* If it were really true that you were a bad person, you could *only* do bad things and could never act morally. This, again, is clearly nonsense, since being a complex, fallible human being, you are likely to act in many different ways, some of which may be moral, some of which may be immoral, and some of which may be morally neutral.

The healthy alternative to this belief is: 'While I was wrong to violate my moral code, I am not a bad person, rather, a fallible human being who did the wrong thing.' This belief is more constructive since it will lead to remorse rather than guilt. Second, it is logical in that it doesn't assume that your act defines your total self, and third, it is consistent with reality, since in reality you are a fallible human being who is a complex mixture of good, bad and neutral.

STEP 7: *Practise your new constructive attitude*. At this point it is likely that you will state that while you can accept intellectually what I have said about challenging your guilt-creating philosophy, it is unlikely that this insight will lead you to feel differently – yet!

As I pointed out in my book *The Incredible Sulk* (Sheldon Press, 1992), in order for you to develop a strong conviction in your new constructive attitudes, which will help you to feel remorse rather than guilt, it is very important for you to practise them. There are a number of ways in which you can do this. First, get accustomed to looking for and identifying your unconstructive attitudes every time you feel guilty. Then, question these unconstructive attitudes in the way I described in Step 6. The more you identify, challenge and respond to these unconstructive attitudes, the more you will come to believe in the more constructive alternative attitudes that are related to remorse.

I want to stress that it is crucial that you do not do this parrot fashion. Really think it through. Write down your guilt-creating attitudes and challenge them using the three questions that I outlined in Step 6. Do this several times a day. Don't copy your previous responses to the three questions. Answer them afresh every time and put your responses in your own words. Really prove to yourself why the guilt-creating attitudes are unconstructive, while the alternative attitudes are more constructive. It is important for you to recognize that this process of questioning your unconstructive guilt-creating attitudes is difficult. However, the more you tolerate this difficulty and persist with this procedure, the more you will become accustomed to it, and the deeper your conviction in the new constructive attitudes will become. As you deepen the conviction, the more you will free yourself from guilt. Unfortunately, however, there is no substitute for repeated practice.

As I discussed in my book *The Incredible Sulk*, there is one specific exercise that you can use which will help you to strengthen your new constructive attitudes and thereby help you to feel healthily remorseful rather than unhealthily guilty. This involves using your imagination.

(1) Write down clearly on a 5″ × 3″ index card the constructive new beliefs that you wish to strengthen.

(2) Imagine, as vividly as possible, the moral code violation about which you feel guilty. Picture your behaviour as clearly as possible.

(3) Allow yourself, temporarily, to experience guilt. This step is important because it takes into account that you will respond initially to a moral code violation with guilt.

(4) As soon as you begin to experience guilt, go over the constructive attitudes on your index card, while still imagining your wrongdoing. Go over these new attitudes as forcefully and as strongly as you can. Don't do it in a weak fashion, since this will not work. Go over these new attitudes strongly until you experience the new healthy feeling of remorse, rather than the unhealthy feeling of guilt. In doing so, you will learn that you can use the feeling of guilt as a cue to think things through more constructively.

Stay with these new constructive attitudes and the corresponding emotion of remorse (while still keeping clearly in mind your wrongdoing) until they begin to feel more natural. Don't expect the new attitudes and the new emotion to feel very natural at first. You will need to practise this exercise many times before you feel at home with them.

I suggest that you practise this imagery exercise three times a day for about ten minutes at a time.

STEP 8: *Re-evaluate your behaviour and learn from your errors.* Once you have helped yourself to feel remorseful about your wrongdoing rather than guilty, you are now in a position to re-evaluate your behaviour and learn from your errors. Ask yourself the question: 'Was my behaviour really as bad as I think it was?' If the answer to this question is yes, you can still learn from your behaviour by reviewing the relevant episode and asking yourself why you think you acted in the way that you did. What was going through your mind at the time which led you to act wrongfully? Your feelings of remorse will help you here. Stay with them until you have understood why you acted in the way you did. Then, you can ask yourself what you can learn from the experience, to minimize the chances of your acting wrongfully in future.

If, however, you come to the conclusion that your action was not as bad as you first thought, or was not a violation of your moral code, you have learned a valuable lesson. You have learned how making yourself feel guilty can cloud your judgement about the badness of your actions.

STEP 9: *Put things right*. If you are still convinced that you have violated your moral code, you are now in a position to think about how to put things right by making amends or planning an act of reparation if appropriate. Since you are no longer feeling guilty, it is unlikely that your attempts to repair the situation will be inappropriate to the situation. It is unlikely, therefore, that you will beg forgiveness from someone whom you have harmed. Rather you ask for forgiveness from that person in an adult-to-adult manner. Also, if you are feeling remorseful rather than guilty, and if you plan to compensate the person for the harm that she suffered (e.g. financially), it is unlikely that you will go over the top and offer a sum of money far more than is appropriate to the situation.

The above nine steps are particularly relevant when the guilt you are experiencing is episodic (i.e. related to a given episode where you acted wrongfully). As you will recall, however, there is another type of guilt called existential guilt. This is the enduring guilt that you experience when you believe that you are bad through and through, not for what you have done, but for who you are. This type of guilt is less responsive to the self-help steps I have just outlined. If you experience this type of guilt I would encourage you to seek professional help. However, let me give you some hints that might help for the time being.

First, consider whether you were scapegoated in your family or ask yourself whether there is any other reason that may explain why you think you are bad through and through. If you can recognize that you were scapegoated in your family, it is important first to work on your anger towards your parents and siblings for scapegoating you. Show yourself that they were fallible human beings who unfortunately did a wrong and unhealthy thing by scapegoating you, and that unfortunately there is no law of the universe which states that they absolutely should not have done the wrong thing (even though it was very wrong). If other members of your family scapegoated you, in all probability they did so because they had emotional problems of their own and they chose to project all their problems onto you instead of dealing with these problems themselves. You need not damn them for this, even though it was very wrong of them to scapegoat you. Keep reminding yourself that they were fallible human beings who acted as they did because they were disturbed, rather than because they were evil wicked people who deserve to be punished.

Second, take the attitude that you are a bad person and show yourself many times that this is completely untrue and unhelpful. If it is true that you are a bad person, everything you ever did in life would be bad and this is extremely unlikely. Even Hitler was kind to animals, to some children, and loved his partner, Eva Braun. So, if Hitler is not a thoroughly bad person, how does it follow that you are? Keep reminding yourself that you are a fallible human being who has learned that you are bad. Show yourself that just because you have the feeling that you are bad does not mean that you are bad. This is a form of emotional reasoning which will keep you trapped in your existential guilt forever. So use your feelings of guilt as a cue to challenge the idea that you are a bad person rather than seeing them as a guide to the truth. This is extremely important, so let me repeat it. Your feelings that you are a bad person are only that, feelings. They are not a guide to reality. What is true is something that you do not believe yet – that you are a fallible human being, who is a complex mixture of good, bad and neutral characteristics. Keep practising this new belief, over and over again, until you start to believe it. Remember that you have probably held the belief that you are bad for as long as you can remember. It will take a lot of practice to shift this idea and to believe that you are a fallible human being like the rest of us. Keep practising the new idea. Act as if it were true. If you do so, I believe it will be worth the effort in the long run.

Index